A BRIEF HISTORY OF ETERNITY

Roy Peacock is a Visiting Professor in the same university in which Galileo worked four hundred years ago. His career has been divided between academic and industrial posts in the UK, Europe and the USA. He played a salient part in research leading to the development of the current generation of Rolls-Royce aero engines and is the author of numerous books.

A Brief History of Eternity is a fascinating story, written from a Christian perspective, of the theories of the universe developed by cosmologists from Aristotle to Hawking. While admitting that the heavens do not prove the existence of God, this book illustrates how they declare his glory.
Don Page, Professor of Physics at Penn State University, USA, and a frequent collaborator with Stephen Hawking.

In the best tradition of C S Lewis — a significant signpost pointing towards the Creator.
John L Wiester, author of *The Genesis Connection*, former President, Astro Industries, Inc.

Roy Peacock shows in this book how there was a beginning and there will be an end to the universe. This must therefore be one of the most significant ways of understanding 'time'. This work will inevitably fuel the controversy about the nature of God and the universe.

Sergei Tarassenko, Nuclear Physicist.

Roy Peacock has written a fascinating historical overview of research scientists' probing of the cosmos, the creation event and the Creator himself.
Dr Hugh Ross, Researcher, California Institute of Technology, President, Reason to Believe.

Professor Peacock has given us an eminently readable survey of the interaction between scientists and their pursuit of the 'how' with the more profound and difficult questions of 'why'. He argues against any temptation to believe that the developments of modern science have in any way detracted from the basic truths of Christian theology.
Richard H. Bube, Professor of Materials Science and Electrical Engineering, Stanford University, California

A Brief History of Eternity

Roy E. Peacock

CROSSWAY BOOKS • WHEATON, ILLINOIS
A DIVISION OF GOOD NEWS PUBLISHERS

To Elizabeth

ACKNOWLEDGEMENTS

The preparation of this book was made the more pleasant and much easier through the enthusiastic support of a number of people. Their help and encouragement are gratefully acknowledged. Some brought wise counsel in offering direction for the writing: in reading the manuscript others were a signal help. Some opened doors into private libraries that might otherwise have remained closed to me: others opened their own libraries and one, on my first visit to him, allowed me to take any material I needed from the shelves of his personal library.

Any views expressed are entirely my own however: for these, together with errors, omissions and other signs of increasing entropy in this manuscript, I am entirely responsible.

Especially, I wish to thank:

His Excellency the British Ambassador to the Holy See, Italy.
Dr. Richard Bube, Stanford University, California, U.S.A.
Rev. George Coyne SJ, Director of the Vatican Observatory, Italy.
Dr. Robert Frost, Escandido, California, U.S.A.
Dr. Walter Hearne, Berkeley, California, U.S.A.
Prof. Renzo Lazzeretti, University of Pisa, Italy.
Dr. Henry Morris, San Diego, California, U.S.A.
Dr. Don Page, Pennsylvania State University, U.S.A.
Dr. Hugh Ross, Pasadena, California, U.S.A.
Dr. Robert Russell, Berkeley, California, U.S.A.
Dr. Carlo Segnini, Director and Librarian, Domus Galilea, Pisa, Italy.
Dr. Sergei Tarassenko, Dorset, U.K.
Dr. Charles Thaxton, Julien, California, U.S.A.

7

Mr. John Wiester, Buellton, California, U.S.A.
The Librarian, Scuola Normale Superiore, Pisa, Italy.
The Library of the Aircraft Research Association, U.K.

I should also like to acknowledge the following for permission to use the illustrations in:
Fig 2.1 By permission of the British Library
Fig 9.1 Photograph reproduced by permission of the Office National D'Etudes et de Recherches Aérospatiales.
Fig 9.2 Photographed by Sadatoshi Taneda and reproduced from *An Album of Fluid Motion* by Milton van Dyke (The Parabolic Press, Stanford, California, USA), fig 94. Copyright owned by Milton van Dyke.

CONTENTS

FOREWORD

I HAVE JUST READ *A Brief History of Eternity* and I recommend it for your reading pleasure and enlightenment. Professor Peacock has done an excellent job of bringing us through the ages to a new understanding of our being.

I did have the opportunity to explore the Apennine mountains of the moon around Hadley Base in the summer of 1971. We performed the famous 'Galileo' gravity experiment by dropping a hammer and a feather at the same instant. It was amazing to see them both fall and contact the moon's surface at the same time. We have come a long way in our search for knowledge of the universe.

We now know and use the laws of the universe. There have been significant changes since the days of Aristotle. I enjoyed the way Professor Peacock brought us to modern scientific thought. I believe science is the understanding of God's basic laws that control the universe.

I was surprised that most of the significant scientists were dedicated Christians. Several years ago I had the pleasure of meeting with Sir Bernard Lovell of Jodrell Bank who shared his Christian faith with me. These brilliant astronomers gave us the vision and understanding of the laws that control our universe. Other Christians who are scientists, like Dr Werner Von Braun, gave us the technology to leave the earth and to travel to other worlds.

We have probed the mysteries of the microcosm with our sophisticated microscopes, and the vastness of the macrocosm with our telescopes. The Hubble telescope is scheduled for launch this year. We continue to ask the question, why? I do know that we must seek the mind of God. Scientists particularly need the mind of God so they might unlock the mysteries of the universe for the benefit of all people. I think that we know what and why God created, but we do not know when or how. The search for truth continues. We have come a long way but there is much more to learn.

Colonel James Irwin
Astronaut

INTRODUCTION

THE COFFEE HOUSES OF LONDON have been meeting places since the late seventeenth century. Samuel Johnson and Samuel Pepys both used them often, as did many others, for discussion, business and argument. It was at one such coffee house in 1684 that a discussion took place between Robert Hooke, the scientist, Edmund Halley, whose name was soon to be associated with the most famous comet of all, and Christopher Wren, the architect. The subject of the conversation was Johannes Kepler.

Kepler, who had died a little over fifty years before, had left a cosmological legacy. Using material gained from his master, Tycho Brahe, from whom he had inherited the most accurate astronomical data available, Kepler had concluded that planetary orbits were elliptical, not circular as tradition demanded, and that the planets travelled at speeds dictated by a curious and apparently unreasonable rule. Why these things should be remained a mystery.

How could Kepler's results be demonstrated mathematically? Hooke said that he could produce the mathematics. Wren didn't believe him. Halley made a wager: a prize for anyone who, in two months, would provide the answer.

Two months later, Hooke had failed, so Halley took the problem to Isaac Newton. By November, a couple of months after Halley's visit to Cambridge, Newton had produced a paper on bodies in orbit, solved the problem and won the prize.

*　　　*　　　*

It was in a coffee house in the Strand, not far from where that wager was made that, 304 years later, I was talking to my publisher. The conversation was far more prosaic. A book of mine had been published three weeks before and now we were looking at several new titles, deciding order, content and timing. As the conversation of the day drew to a close, a comment was made, rather as an aside, about Stephen Hawking's book *A Brief History of Time*. Little was said at that meeting beyond an observation on the mathematical model of a universe with no boundary in the spacetime frame. This fired my interest and, as I read the book, comparing it with comments circulating about it, my thoughts on the matter were also fired. From that there grew a series of discussions with scientists — physicists and cosmologists who had themselves thought deeply on the subject of the universe, its origins and its destiny. Without exception, every one encouraged me to put my thoughts in writing.

The result is this book.

From antiquity, many men have claimed that the universe was everlasting — having neither beginning nor end. But I knew, as a scientist, that such claims did not harmonise with my understanding of scientific principles, particularly those things I had learned as a thermodynamicist. Science is broad in concept and application, yet it is fascinating to discover that the laws learned in one area are not contravened in another: to that extent, science is one. It means that any one area of science is accessible, at least in part, from the experience and discipline of any other. And it is this convergence to which I have appealed in this book.

The task has had its challenges. Cosmology is expressed in the language of mathematics, responding to the principles of theoretical and particle physics. It is restrained by the laws of mechanics, but also obeys the legal requirements of the laws of thermodynamics. In all of these disciplines, the scientist communicates in his own language, a shorthand in which one technical word or term, honed to precision, carries an understanding that requires half a paragraph to explain. How does the writer express himself; in an esoteric language that admits only the few to knowledge, or with full, ponderous, definitions using yards of script and lulling the reader to sleep?

Communication is a problem — the Englishman abroad merely shouts louder to be understood by a non-English speaking audience, but the attitude of the scientist generally is possibly even worse: he doesn't communicate at all except with those who trouble to learn his language. Over the doors of Plato's school were inscribed the words, 'Let no one ignorant of geometry enter here' and, while it probably made good sense, it represented a division between an élitist group and all the others. To defend this principle Nicholas Copernicus warned, in the preface to his great work that set in motion the Copernican theory, 'Mathematics is for mathematicians.'

Galileo Galilei, who figures in my book, recognised the problem. In speaking of reading the book of nature, the cosmos, he said, 'But it cannot be read unless one first learns to comprehend the language and read the letters in which it is composed. It is written in the language of mathematics ... without which it is humanly impossible to understand a single word of it.' Yet it was Galileo who infuriated the academic establishment of the day by writing his major works, not in the language of scholarship, Latin, but in Italian. He did so because he wanted to reach an audience which, 'being unable to read things written in Latin, become convinced that ... the latest discoveries of logic and philosophy must remain forever over their heads. Now, I want them to see that just as nature has given them as well as the philosophers, eyes to see her works, so she has also given them brains capable of grasping and understanding them.' Galileo wrote so that the world could understand — and it did.

In attempting to do the same thing, I may have lost some of the precision of science's language. Peers may consider that science is being prostituted and the non-scientist may feel that I have still failed to achieve effective communication. You must be the judge.

What is the aim of my book? At the end of *A Brief History of Time* Stephen Hawking poses a series of questions. 'What is it that breathes fire into the equations and makes a universe for them to describe? The usual approach of science of constructing a mathematical model cannot answer the questions of why there should be a universe for the model to describe. Why does the universe go to all the bother of existing? Is the unified theory so compelling that it brings about its own existence? Or does it need a creator, and if so, does he have any other effect on the universe? And who created him?' These are the questions that drive Hawking and are left unanswered. I attempt to address them — or at least as many as are addressable.

I do so, not by building mathematical models: Hawking concludes that that is unfruitful. Nor do I try to develop a causal relationship between the mechanics behind the construction of the universe and the reason why it is there. How it got there and how it works make for fascinating study. Maybe close investigation reveals a set of fingerprints that show it has all been carefully handled, but no more. Yet the giants of science, thinking in a vacuum bounded only by the experience of their forebears, had something else to say. They were interested in how the cosmos works and hence how it originated, but they, like us, also wanted to know why. Many of them found out, and that is our eventual focus. As Hawking puts it, this is knowing the mind of God — and that is the ultimate goal in all science.

CHAPTER ONE

HOW OR WHY?

MY FIRST SIGHT of Saturn was sensational. Before that, I hadn't much interest in the heavens. My son had been totally immersed in astronomy as a hobby for some time but, like chicken-pox, his disease was catching — and I was in danger of catching it. Until that evening, Saturn had been just another luminous pin-prick — one among many that I couldn't identify without detailed direction from a teenage zealot.

But this night was different. Following several hints by my son, I had previously bought him a telescope as a present for good grades at school. This was no ordinary eye-glass, like Nelson's. It was, I was told, a Newtonian reflector which meant that a system of mirrors produced a more impressive result. It also produced a more impressive bill when the mirrors were resilvered! So there we were as darkness fell on a cold clear evening, with a refurbished telescope on top of a slight hill in the English countryside, a few miles North of Luton Airport. I had been handed a pair of binoculars to look through and keep me from grumbling about the temperature — in England, astronomy is a cold sport — and had spent some time, as instructed, trying to focus on a blob of light in the sky: the light remained fuzzy to the eye but did appear to be other than round.

We had made the mistake of setting up the quite impressively sized, white-painted telescope at the side of a little-used road. That night, though, an almost continuous stream of traffic had been diverted along it. The specialist of the party gave instructions that we should look away from any car headlights lest our 'night vision' was destroyed.

My son's exclamation of triumph as he focused on Saturn

immediately had me elbowing my way to the eyepiece of the telescope.

There it was. Pictures and drawings abound, most of which contain far greater detail than we could ever see through a six inch Newtonian telescope, but nothing compared to seeing the real thing. It wasn't a good night for viewing. There was too much turbulence in the atmosphere, I was told: that was why the picture kept going in and out of focus. But that made the moments of clear sight the more amazing. There were the rings, and there were their shadows on the surface of the planet; and every now and again, Cassini's division, the black gap separating the inner from the outer rings. I was hooked.

It was similar to another night when I first saw the moons of Jupiter. Here was history being lived out: four centuries before, Galileo had looked through his telescope at these same moons. He had discovered the key that had unlocked the fact of a cosmos whose centre was not the earth, had justified Copernicus, branded Galileo as a heretic and had closed the file on Ptolemy and Aristotle. It was just this view in my eye-piece that had disposed with a geometry of the universe and a philosophy which had put man at its centre.

Galileo's telescope still exists in Florence: its lens is cracked. Through mishandling, his character has also been flawed. He has been branded as an enemy of the church as well as lionised as the prophet of a new age of thinking. It is said that his was a battle with a religious system. His observations were to free men from the power of religiously minded demagogues, reactionaries against any advancement in mankind. Because of Galileo, a medieval fear of the authority of the church was broken.

For a moment I shared Galileo's excitement as he had squinted through his eye-piece, although his elation must have grown with time as he traced the passage of four moons around their parent planet which happened not to be the earth.

Not only was I observing elements that changed man's thinking, I had been looking at a mystery that has been a fascination from the beginning of time, and reflected upon man's understanding of his origins, his philosophy and his religion. The movement of the planets had been accurately timed, the heavens were carefully mapped, their mechanics had been established and refined, but there was still a mystery. Why was it all there and why were we here? How it worked was a still unfolding discovery, a triumph of intuitive thinking and intellectual ability. How it had begun was the subject of conjecture, scientifically and mathematically expressed: compelling for that, with an authority inherent in its technical presentation, but still conjecture.

Two types of investigation are commonly used to discover the *how* of the origins of the universe. The first is to establish what it is doing now: is it expanding, static or contracting? From this, the cosmologist extrapolates backwards in time, using the laws of physics to reach an initiating point.

Problems emerge. The first is that it is not really possible to say that, if the universe is currently expanding — which it is — it has therefore always expanded in much the same manner. What if the universe actually pulsed, repeated expansions and contractions such as we see in a beating heart, although at vastly different frequency? The scientist knows that extrapolation always has its difficulties: this highlights them.

Then there is another problem in tracing the history of the universe backwards. If there was a starting point, it occurred at what mathematicians call a singularity. Now a singularity is a perplexing thing. It is a point at which all the known laws no longer apply: they break down. Thus we have an embarrassing situation: we use our laws to go back to the early moments of the universe, but the very aids we have to get us there cannot complete the job and we have nothing else to hand.

The second approach is to search for any residual evidence of the starting moment. Is there a smoking gun out there, maybe an echo of a Big Bang — a primordial explosion of enormous proportions that began the whole process of which we are part? Could such an echo still be reverberating through space, like a bell continuing to ring a long time after it has been struck?

Maybe that echo has been found. A microwave radiation — energy whose form is similar to that used in a microwave oven — of very low intensity, but of uniform strength in every direction, was accidently detected some years ago. It was so faint that the observers assumed at first that their detector, a microwave collector intended for a quite different investigation, was not working properly. It had already been suggested that, if there had been a Big

Bang, such radiation might be found. It had, but inadvertently! But pressing as the evidence was, it was still circumstantial.

Difficulties surround the investigation of an event which might have occurred a long time ago, using rules that are invalid at the crucial moment and observations whose relevance is circumstantial. An alternative philosophy therefore becomes very attractive. There is one: assume that there was no beginning! The immediate advantage is that the singularity denying the use of our scientific laws has been dismissed. Instead, as we shall see, other problems are introduced.

The concept of an everlasting cosmos is not new. Aristotle's view of this was clear when he introduced his unchanging universe. No change meant that nothing could have started things off — there could have been no development leading to the heavens as he saw them. By the same argument, it could be judged that a universe having no beginning would have no end. Man's place was assured for all time, a comforting thought.

Interestingly, the notion of no end and no beginning to the universe has reappeared nearly two and a half thousand years later with the Stephen Hawking model proposed in his book *A Brief History of Time*. Hawking's proposition is supported by a mathematical model of ingenious construction and interpretation. Aristotle could afford no such luxury: he just presumed it to be so because, as the earth appeared to be immovable, nothing else within his scientific gaze, other than the planets and the stars beyond which circulated periodically, was on the move either.

But even if the greatest mystery for which detectives have sought clues — *how* did the universe begin? — was answered, it wouldn't begin to explain *why*. The question of the enquiring scientist may be *how*? His training has prepared him to probe nature in this way and honed him so that he can weigh up the possible answers. Yet the world's instinctive question is not *how* but *why*? Why did the earthquake, resulting in such loss of life, happen? Why was that friend killed in the accident? Why did my career go the way it did? And with the *why* there is an implicit appeal to forces that may control the events of life.

The *why* goes beyond the draughtsmanship of the heavens: it is in a different dimension to the physics and chemistry of processes that have led to the pattern of things we see. It is a philosophical question insufficiently addressed in unlocking the secrets of the cosmos and its beginning.

Science is simply a knowledge of what *is*. Its primary concern is with facts, not motives: motives can't be handled in a laboratory as an ingredient in an experiment. Yet the motive behind what *is* usually harmonises with the facts, otherwise forensic examination by the police would be a waste of time. At best though, the discovery of what *is* may identify the fingerprint of the originator.

And the scientist doesn't have much else to go on. So the gleanings from cosmology and cosmogony do have an application: the sciences whose laws controlled everything viewed through my son's telescope and beyond its horizon, are put to use.

* * *

The search for an understanding of how the heavens work and how the cosmos got there in the first place is an intriguing story. It is one of logic and intuition, of politics and personal vendetta — and of detective work whose results vied with long-held, if largely mistaken ideas. We shall see how theories were deemed respectable and hence beyond challenge, just because they were old, established and had never been challenged. In particular, the story is about two directly opposed schools of thought, one of which held the earth as the centre of the universe — a geography giving man a special place in the scheme of things, and the other in which the earth was not at the centre. Further, it is a story that shows the efforts of scientists to reconcile experimental observation and mathematical model, a synthesis held back by prejudice — blind spots in the otherwise clear minds of great men. It is also the story of one planet, Mars, whose trajectory stubbornly refused to agree with a succession of models but whose apparently eccentric behaviour was the spur to find a mathematical solution matching the observable mechanics of the universe.

As is often the case in scientific history, no individual made the ultimate breakthrough, if it has ever been made. But we see a series of minds, each with its own special strengths as well as weaknesses and each building upon the advances of a predecessor. Isaac Newton, one of this illustrious chain, said, 'If I have seen further than others, it is because I have stood on the shoulders of giants.' The lineage includes Aristotle, Ptolemy, Copernicus, Brahe,

Kepler and then Newton. It continues with Faraday, Clerk-Maxwell and Einstein. And since the quest is not yet over, the list has yet to be completed.

To readers in the late twentieth century, the steps of these men may seem obvious. Of course we know that as the moon revolves around the earth, the earth revolves around the sun, that the sun is a minor star in an outer suburb of a galaxy we call the Milky Way and that the Milky Way is one of innumerable galaxies. We know these things, not because we have checked them for ourselves, but because we have been told them and time has made them respectable.

But this has not always been the case. A rotating earth was a nonsense to people who didn't feel it moving. To them, a fixed earth was an entirely reasonable assumption. It was equally reasonable to conclude that all else in the heavens moved about the earth. In this climate, the first suggestion that our bit of the universe was not immovably fixed was epoch-making.

The idea of a mobile earth was, therefore, counter to the received scientific thinking of the day. But it was also in contradiction with the perceived religious prejudices of that time. That is not to say that these pioneers were irreligious or non-religious men, people whose advancement of scientific understanding put them outside the pale of the church. Rather the reverse is true, for in those who broke the mould of Aristotle's cosmological model, from Copernicus to Clerk-Maxwell, we shall find men who recognised a fingerprint on creation and ascribed it to the God they worshipped.

For these fathers of science, the world and its life was not divided into two warring camps, science and Christianity. There was a synthesis that they understood, put into words by Kepler when he exclaimed, 'O God, I am thinking thy thoughts after thee.' It is the synthesis that Stephen Hawking seeks as he concludes that when we know the why of the universe, we shall know the mind of God.

That is the reason for the *why* — and why the question is intrinsic to man. Tracing the footsteps of great men we shall discover it to be a theme to which they return as certainly as a compass needle continuously seeks magnetic North. It is a question that lurks behind every step made in cosmology, and it demands an answer.

We shall also discover that no science exists in isolation. Science does not comprise a number of self-sufficient systems of cause and effect. All areas of science interact, at some point, with all others. None has rules of operation that contradict any other area so, while every field has identifying characteristics, a tight interdependence results among scientific disciplines.

In the areas of scientific endeavour, cosmology is unique: the experiment giving the observations to check cosmological thinking is the largest conceivable — everything created comes within the domain of the cosmologist. But in other ways cosmology is not unique. It must appeal to the laws and conventions of other branches of science for its expression. Without the observations gained from astronomy, the cosmologist would have no material with which to work. Without mathematics as the main descriptive tool, he would soon run out of words to discuss or develop his arguments. Without the fundamentals of physics as we know them, he would have no framework within which to operate and no constraint upon his most extravagant ideas.

In particular, as we shall discover in chapter 4, the laws of thermodynamics, primary in the world of physics, reign supreme in cosmology as they do in any branch of science in which a process is involved. And from the time that Tycho Brahe watched a supernova in November 1572 — an exploding star in the constellation Cassiopeia — it was recognised that changes, processes, occurred in the heavens. The cosmos did not present the static, unchanging and unchangeable picture that Aristotle had assumed nearly two thousand years before. Processes meant that energy was involved. Energy dictated that thermodynamics played its vital part. Thermodynamics spoke of two unchanging laws of the universe to which all else would submit. Chapter 4 explores these in some detail.

It is this submission to the overarching science of thermodynamics that is important in this book. As we apply the plumbline of the Second Law in particular, many ideas will necessarily be abandoned and others will be fortified.

This aspect of science does not take us into the rarified atmosphere of theoretical physics. Although expressing the laws of thermodynamics was the climbing of an intellectual Everest, their application is entirely prosaic. Everyday life answers to these laws.

The First Law operates in every fireplace in the world and the Second Law determines how often we need to put fuel into our vehicles. In fact, the consequences of the operation of these two laws are so commonplace that if they were ever to be disobeyed, everybody would notice it — not just the thermodynamicist who can recite the laws and put figures into calculations supporting them. People would remark that something was not right. If, to keep a fire burning, we had continually to take lumps of coal off, or to run our cars we needed regularly to remove fuel from the fuel tank — a picture akin to running a film in reverse — then it would be cause for comment and a collapse of the stock market dealing in shares in oil companies!

It is remarkable that the rules describing a boiling kettle also describe the way the sun gives us heat. They decide the changes taking place everywhere our telescopes can look. Further, their operation is from the time immediately after any Big Bang to that of any final whimper of the universe. So far as we can judge, the laws of thermodynamics are ultimately reliable: they can be depended upon. The reliability in *de*scription leads to their use in *pre*scription. Because the kettle has always boiled when heated for long enough, we say that the kettle always will boil if heated for long enough.

And this is why we refer to the cosmos as the universe: all things created or existing constitute a systematic whole. It has all been turned into one by the observations we make and the rules that result. The rules are, then, applicable anywhere at any time — except perhaps at the moment of initiation itself. This is the great cosmological conundrum: laws whose job is to describe the operation of all that we know in the universe don't actually apply to the beginning of the story. We shall be looking at this in chapter 6 and will see how it becomes the spur to considering a universe without beginning — a new picture but with the shadow of Aristotle cast upon it.

*   *   *

Even if we find that the laws of thermodynamics give a good, consistent and entirely agreeable picture of the operation of the universe and, further, yield an understanding about the beginning — should there have been one — we would still have done nothing other than describe the *how* of the universe. The *why* would continue to be conjecture gained from the *how*. I might watch my neighbour digging his garden. Perhaps I can understand how he does it, using the muscles of arms and legs so that the spade is thrust into the ground and the soil is turned over. But I don't know why he is doing it. Maybe where he is digging and the way he works the soil suggests to me that he is going to plant potatoes or maybe rose trees. Unless I ask him though, I am guessing. If he tells me that he is intending to bury his nosey next-door neighbour I must conclude that the evidence has yielded to me the wrong answer — the *how* had not led to the *why*, and the conjecture is wrong.

This book will not shed the ultimate light on the early universe. What it will do is to separate what is unlikely from what is likely in our thinking. It will do so by indicating areas of conflict between some current ideas and the consequences of these laws. But the book will do something else. Having pointed the reader away from the unlikely to the likely it will take us beyond the *how*, for the likely gives us a clue to the *why*. That, after all, means that we are addressing the most basic question.

CHAPTER TWO

COSMOS REVIEWED: A PATH TO DETERMINISM

IT'S COMMON SENSE to think of the earth as immovable. It seems fixed beneath our feet because we don't feel it moving: therefore we say it is fixed. This is what led Aristotle to his system for the universe. Because the earth was stationary, he said, everything he could see moving — the sun, moon and the planets — necessarily revolved around the earth. Those bodies that didn't

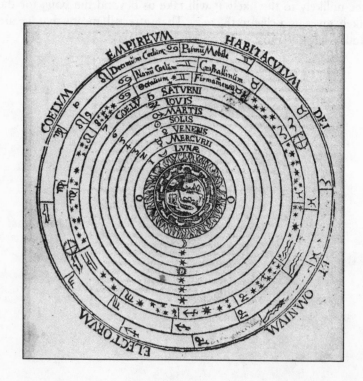

seem to move relative to one another were fixed on a sphere, revolving once a day, that surrounded the earth at some great distance. Thus Aristotle's picture of the universe was one with a focus in an immovable earth and around this everything rotated in a series of circular orbits — a vast celestial clockwork [Fig 2.1].

The idea of circular motion was based, not upon any scientific observation, merely in prevailing Greek philosophical insistence that a circle was a perfect shape, so motion should therefore be

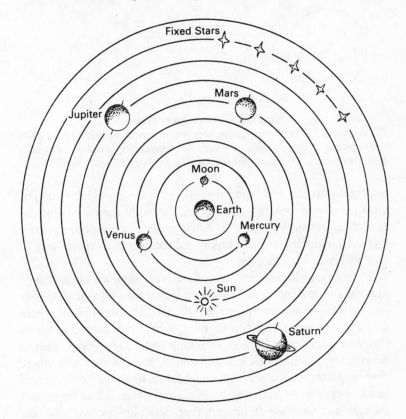

Fig 2.1a & b The Aristotelian Universe
An earth-centred universe, proposed by Aristotle, was generally held to be true until the sixteenth century, although there were some early Greek philosophers who thought that the sun should be considered as central. This is a sixteenth-century drawing giving the relative positions of the planets around which there was a sphere of stars, rotating once a day. No attempt was made to portray the distances between the various orbits.

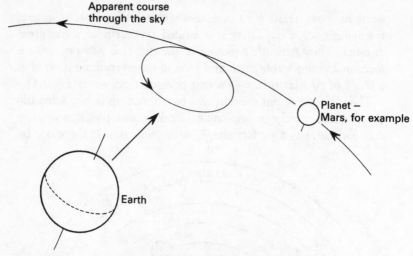

Fig 2.2 The Wandering of Planets
The direction of planetary movement, seen from the earth, is reversed for a while
before returning to the original direction. This 'wandering' posed a challenge to
Aristotle's system. The reason for the phenomenon is explained in fig 2.4.

uniformly circular and thus appropriate for the grand panorama of
universe spread before the observer. Aristotle therefore saw the
planets as embedded in a concentric series of crystalline spheres,
layered like the leaves of an onion and rotating in a regular way as
they slid over one another.

Aristotle developed some other fundamental views. He reckoned
that the sun and moon were 'perfect' lights. He said that all bodies
had 'natural movement' propelling them to a 'natural place' where
they came to rest. On the earth, then, light bodies moved upwards
(fire is the example he had in mind) and heavy bodies moved
downwards, like a brick being dropped, because that was where
they found their natural places. In addition, heavenly bodies stayed
in the heavens — that was their natural place. Most important
though and because it looked that way, he decreed that the
universe was unchanging. If it never changed, it followed that it
would never end, and this also meant that it never began. The
universe always was, its existence stretching back and forward an
infinite time.

But Aristotle's physics had problems. While it was conceptually
simple, the movement of planets didn't actually correspond to his

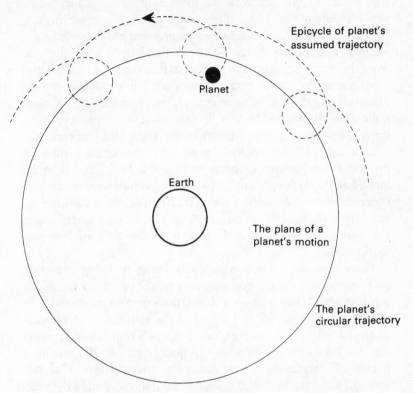

Fig 2.3 Epicycles

To account for the wandering of planets, a system of epicycles was introduced. These are circles traced out while moving along a line in a manner similar to a particle on, say, the flange of a railway wheel as it is moving along a track. While the method appeared to give adequate predictions of planetary position, it could not explain the phenomenon in physical terms.

dictate of uniform motion in circular orbits. There was a so-called wandering of planets, an erratic movement in which they appeared to stop their progress across the sky and go backwards for a short while before continuing in their original direction [Fig 2.2]. In an attempt to correct for this, dodges were introduced. The circle, being the perfect shape, was retained, but circular trajectories were superimposed on other circular trajectories — so-called epicycles — to make the mathematics agree with observation [Fig 2.3]. The perfect match of observation with prediction was elusive, and this was especially the case with the movement of the planet Mars, which eventually became the greatest problem to astronomers.

In due course, Ptolemy inherited the problem of Mars. He finally adopted a desperate dodge — he put the earth a short distance from the centre of planetary rotation so that the orbit of Mars and other planets became eccentric to the earth. This produced a means of calculating the odd behaviour of planetary motion and worked quite well. His method became known as the Ptolemaic system. By now, Aristotle's system of concentric crystalline spheres was abandoned — they couldn't cope with the strange motions proposed. But Ptolemy's scheme had the disadvantage that, when looked at closely, very complex planetary motions were required, a contradiction of Aristotle's claim that nature always did things the easy way. In spite of this, Ptolemy's work was unchallenged for nearly fourteen hundred years until the time of Nicholas Copernicus.

There had been much argument relating to fixing planetary position: should the method only be a means of calculating where a planet was at any time — a cinematic system — or should it be descriptive of how things worked in the universe — a physical system? Looked at in another way, Ptolemy's system clearly didn't describe the mechanics of what was going on, but it did provide a means of calculating where heavenly bodies were. Was this enough? Copernicus thought not, and for good reason. In the years that had elapsed, small errors in Ptolemy's method had accumulated and it had been necessary to put in corrections which themselves were in error.

Copernicus therefore had a mission: he was determined to produce a cosmological method that was physically possible, truly descriptive of what went on in the heavens. Unfortunately, he was also determined to employ circular orbits for the planets, the consequence of centuries of established thinking.

A lifetime of mathematical investigation led Copernicus to one staggering conclusion — the earth was not at a universal centre around which everything rotated. It moved in its own orbit. The wanderings of the planets could be explained in that the observer, himself on the earth, moved in an orbit like the planets, but at his own, different, rate [Fig 2.4]. Rather like the passenger in one car watching the movement of another, the observer saw the

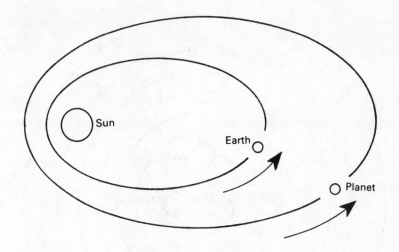

Fig 2.4 Planetary Orbits

Orbits are elliptical and planetary speeds vary as indicated in fig 2.7. In addition, the time of a planetary cycle (its year) depends on its orbit. The wandering of planets is due to the relative speed differences of planets being observed from a moving planet.

relative speed and position of the object, not the absolute speed and position. So the earth moved and Copernicus concluded that its movement was around the sun: this, and not the earth, was the focus for revolution of the planets [Fig 2.5]. His solution was breath-taking in vision, elegant in concept and unrealistic in the experience of people who had always said the earth didn't move because they didn't feel it moving. At least Aristotle's and Ptolemy's schemes had appealed to common sense: this did not.

Copernicus had two problems. The first arose from his insistence upon circular orbits. The apparently simple motions of the planets needed modification and the resultant mathematics was as complicated as Ptolemy's — and hardly more accurate. Ptolemy had been able to predict the position of Mars with an error of a little over 5°; Copernicus to a little under 5°. This was to remain a problem until the two-thousand-year-old tradition of circular orbits — inherited from the school of Pythagoras whose shadow still casts gloom over schoolboys — was broken.

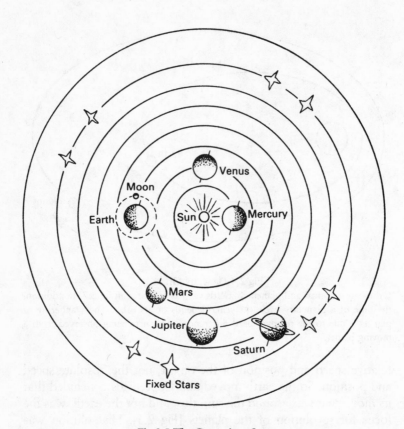

Fig 2.5 The Copernican System
While he still thought that planetary motion was circular, Copernicus made the
vital step of proposing a sun-centred system. This figure is taken from *De
Revolutionibus* and shows the order of the planets. Uranus, Neptune and Pluto do
not figure since they weren't discovered until 1781, 1846 and 1930 respectively.

And there was a second problem. Not only was Copernicus
afraid that his scheme would be ridiculed because it didn't appeal
to common sense, it might also be rejected by the church. As a
Christian and a canon in the church, he was well aware of the
church's traditional thinking and the grip this had. But Copernicus
was also a lawyer, an efficient administrator and, in thought and
action, evidently a politician. Accordingly, he reported his work
circumspectly. He mentioned his reluctance to publish, but that
this had been overcome by the persuasion of friends, one of whom

happened to be a bishop and the other a cardinal! He was careful not to claim originality for his scheme — he had in fact learned Greek especially to read early and untranslated Greek writings on the subject — and cited no less than four Greek mathematicians who had argued for the mobility of the earth. Then he had extolled the unique nature of the sun to make its new-found position more acceptable. Sensing that an attack might come from traditionalists in the church, he made a pre-emptive strike — 'if there are idle talkers who take it upon themselves to pronounce judgement, although wholly ignorant of mathematics and if by shamelessly distorting the sense of some passage of Holy Writ to suit their purpose, they dare to reprehend and attack my work, they worry me so little that I shall even scorn their judgements as foolhardy. Mathematics is written for mathematicians.' Finally, he added the cap-stone to his thesis: he dedicated it to the Pope!

Even so, Copernicus was slow to publish and it was only on his death-bed that he first held in his hand a printed copy of his great work *De Revolutionibus*. Many of his ideas were to be superseded as advances were made, but Copernicus made to astronomy one contribution whose influence cannot be overstressed — he removed the sun from the category of a planet and put it as the focus of his system. The earth was relegated to being one of several bodies orbiting around a parent — it was no longer at the centre of things.

Copernicus had failed to improve on Ptolemy's accuracy although he had wanted to get within 10 minutes of arc (⅙th of a degree) of available measurements, a futile target since measurements were not themselves that accurate. But this was all changed by a Danish astronomer, Tycho Brahe, whose observations were at least thirty times more accurate than any before him. Without the benefit of a telescope (not yet invented) Brahe produced positional tables of high accuracy. To do so involved designing new instruments and introducing scientific procedures that have been used ever since. So accurate were his observations that he recorded tiny irregularities in the moon's motion which remained unexplained until Isaac Newton's time.

Brahe was a colourful person, a nobleman who had had his nose cut off in a duel and, as a result, wore one made of metal. His plans to be a philosopher abruptly changed in 1550 when he saw an eclipse of the sun. It wasn't just the fact of the eclipse that impressed him, it was that it had been predicted. From this moment, astronomy became his life.

Two of Brahe's observations are of particular importance. In the fixed stars he saw no parallax, changes in the relative positions of the stars which, he reasoned, should be observed if the earth moved in space. We see the same effect in telling the time from a clock. Because the hands stand proud of the dial, they appear to point to different dial marks if we move our position from one side of the clock to the other. In the same way, two stars at different distances from us would appear to alter their relative position as we moved. Brahe concluded that with no parallax, the earth did not move relative to the fixed stars. What he did not realise was that they were so distant that the effect was immeasurably small. Nevertheless, this idea of a fixed earth was reinforced for Brahe by his interpretation of the Bible which, to him, seemed to indicate an immovable earth.

In consequence, Tycho Brahe developed a new model for the universe, a hybrid of the Copernican model in which everything rotated around the sun and the Ptolemaic model which had a stationary earth. It was never generally accepted.

Another of Brahe's major observations is recorded in his diary for 1572. 'One evening when I was contemplating, as usual, the celestial vault, I saw, with inexpressible astonishment, near the zenith, in Cassiopeia, a radiant star of extra-ordinary magnitude.' To this diligent observer, who had measured slight perturbations in the Moon's trajectory and for whom the plan of the heavens was a familiar sight, a new light that dominated the sky must have been stunning. Brahe had seen a supernova — a star exploding in its death process. The observation destroyed the dictate of Aristotle that the universe never altered. Things did change and that change, the death of a star, would in due course be recognised as a process of decay.

With declining health, Brahe took an assistant, a young mathematician named Johannes Kepler. In the face of great personal affliction, Kepler was destined to solve the great riddle of universal motion, releasing the grip of a Greek philosophy that saw perfection in simple geometric shapes.

Researchers are individualists, people who live in the private world of their own thoughts, interacting with others only in so far as it helps their work. The popular picture of the absent-minded professor is often not so far from the truth — a new secretary fled from my office once when I appeared from behind my desk without my shoes, having forgotten to put them on — and a very forgetful Cambridge colleague's lecture notes which had prompts to remind him to pause for the audience's laughter were a sight to behold! Knowing his morose demeanour, I sometimes thought that the pauses must have been dramatic — and long! The process of life can be an annoying and destructive diversion to the man who is in pursuit of a discovery.

Kepler's record is an outstanding story of triumph in adversity. For most of his life he was close to illness. He was bodily weak and from a child suffered almost continuously with bad health. Three of the four children of his first marriage died followed by his wife, whose death through typhus was only months after that of the last son. Five children of his second marriage also died in infancy. He was often not paid by his employers and endured personal hardship for that. He was surrounded by war, political and religious friction and, because of his clear Christian commitment, had secure academic posts denied him. His Christian faith also cost him the security of his home in Graz and, in turn, was the reason for him having to flee from Prague, then Linz and finally Sagan.

Yet in all this, as well as the extraordinary achievements he made in astronomy, he saw the hand of God: after all, Graz had led to Prague where he had formed the valuable relationship with Tycho Brahe.

Kepler needed Brahe, or rather, he needed Brahe's meticulously measured data of planetary and stellar positions. In his own words, Kepler's aim in life was to 'transfer the whole of astronomy from fictitious circles to natural causes'. He wasn't interested in refining geometrical techniques to describe the movement of the planets but to find the actual physical causes of the motions. There was no use, to him, in constructing a model that didn't agree with the best data on offer.

But it was hardly on offer. In the tradition of scientists down through the ages, Brahe was suspicious of Kepler's motives. The researcher wants nothing less than total secrecy for his work in the

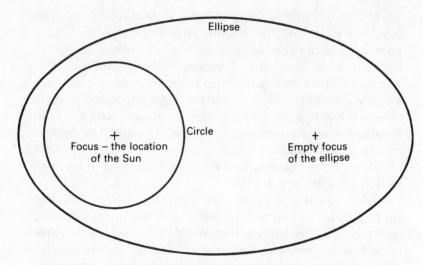

Fig 2.6 The Elliptical Orbit
This figure exaggerates the different shapes of circular and elliptical orbits. The orbits of planets close to the sun are almost circular, but Kepler's discovery of the elliptical pattern was vital in freeing the Copernican system from the epicycles it had inherited from the earth-centred model.

making so that there is no plagiarism of the world-shaking material he has. Then he wants nothing less than total exposure of the data the moment it is published with his name on it. Nevertheless, Brahe knew that his health would not hold out until the publication of his work.

It didn't and he didn't. Within a year of joining him, Kepler saw Brahe die. Kepler's response typifies the man, 'God let me be bound to Tycho through an unalterable fate and did not let me be separated from him.'

Having been encouraged by Brahe on his deathbed to complete his tabulated data, Kepler thus inherited the best measurements history had. With them, he also inherited the problem of Mars! Between Tycho's observations — known to have an accuracy of within 1 minute of arc — and the Ptolemaic calculation was an error of 8 minutes, negligible by the standards of a previous generation but big enough in Kepler's eyes to be the spur for his research and, as we shall see, to be the cause of the great revolution science was to see.

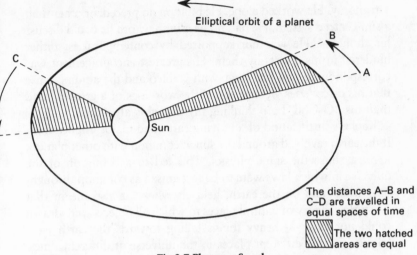

Fig 2.7 Planetary Speed

Kepler discovered that the rule governing planetary speed declared that in equal intervals of time, equal areas would be swept in the elliptical orbit as indicated in this figure. The reason for this was the subject of the wager between Halley, Hooke and Wren: the solution was discovered by Newton.

For four years, and without the benefit of computers, calculators and, for most of the time, even without tables of logarithms which John Napier was busily inventing in Scotland, Kepler did calculation after calculation in an attempt to get the match he needed. It was in 1605, eleven years after he had set out on his personal voyage of discovery in the mathematics of astronomy, that he noticed his successive sketches of orbits pointed towards an elliptical shape [Fig 2.6]. Having established an ellipse, an elongated circle, as the path for a planet, Kepler then addressed the problem of the variation in speed that it would have in its rotation. In this, he discovered a law that was conceptually perplexing and had no obvious principle in physics: the area swept by a line joining the sun and a planet within the ellipse of the planet's orbit was always the same for an equal interval of time [Fig 2.7]. The principle behind this and the other laws Kepler discovered remained to be described in Newton's laws of motion.

Although he described himself as a Copernican, Kepler destroyed all but the sun-centred pattern of Copernicus' scheme when he proposed an entirely new basis for the dynamics of astronomy. He worked alone. He built on no precedent other than a sun-centred system. He had no peer with whom he could discuss his thoughts. He was not supported by contemporaries, rather hindered in his efforts by them. His greatest encouragement was correspondence at a late stage with Galileo and the abiding sense that his discoveries were to reveal the workings of a greater mind than his. 'O God, I am thinking thy thoughts after thee.'

Kepler's justification of a moving earth had major implications. If the earth revolved around the sun in common with other planets, it must share the same physics. This led to a definition of the universe in which laws were to be recognised as common throughout: what held on the earth, held elsewhere. It also meant that Aristotle's theory of natural places to which all objects were drawn could not exist — heavy things falling towards the earth were falling towards different places in the universe at different times, since the earth was itself moving.

Johannes Kepler stood at the threshold of a new science. Stripped of its Greek mythology and a philosophy that looked for cinematic (that is, representative of the movement) rather than physical likeness, here was a descriptive method portraying the physics and giving good agreement between observation and theory. This became the philosophical basis for all subsequent scientific endeavour.

Looking back, Kepler recognised the importance of the apparent error in the position of Mars, giving honour where honour was due, 'Divine Providence granted us such a diligent observer in Tycho Brahe that his observations convicted the Ptolemaic calculation of an error of 8 minutes. It is only right that we should accept God's gift with a grateful mind. Because these 8 minutes could not be ignored, they alone have led to a total reformation in astronomy.'

Kepler published his findings in 1609.

*   *   *

The years 1609 and 1610 were, for astronomy, two of the most important in history, not only because of Kepler's publication in Germany but because of a series of reports coming from Padua, a city near Venice in northern Italy. The story, however, has two beginnings, one in Holland and the other in Pisa in Italy.

Some report that it was Hans Lippershey, the spectacle maker, others that it was Jacobus Metius who made the discovery. In any event, Holland was the location of one of those accidents that has major — and in this case — beneficial repercussions.

Making spectacles involves handling lenses which need to be checked and this includes looking through them. It was during such an examination that the spectacle maker found himself looking through not one, but two lenses. To his surprise, the magnification of the lens combination was much greater than that of a single lens. In placing the two lenses at opposite ends of a tube to locate them more firmly, the telescope was invented. News of this remarkable device spread quickly across Europe and soon reached Galileo Galilei, Professor of mathematics at the University of Padua.

Galileo was a man with wide interests. He was, above all, an experimenter looking to harmonise the observations of experimental physics and the supporting mathematics, something that Aristotle's approach failed to do. Galileo had been born in Pisa, whose Leaning Tower is reputed to have played some part in his investigations into mechanics. His formative years, from the age of ten to seventeen, were spent in Florence in the midst of the ferment of the Renaissance. He returned to Pisa as a student in medicine where the free-thinking he had found natural in the Florentine Renaissance was not encouraged. His independent character ran counter to accepted norms and, after three years, he left Pisa without a degree. Interestingly this independence of thought proved to be the vital ingredient for the genius he was and also the efficient means of making the enemies he had.

His dedication to medicine waned and by the time that, in 1589, he returned to Pisa as Professor in mathematics, Galileo's fertile mind had already ranged over other subjects. One of these involved a question that had taxed scientists over many years — a brain teaser of the type that keeps university common-room conversation from being totally moribund. A king had a crown made in gold, but it was suspected that the goldsmith had adulterated the gold with the inclusion of some silver. Without defacing the crown in the examination, how could it be shown if silver had been alloyed with the gold — and if so, how much? Galileo proposed a new form of balance to weigh the crown. Not

Fig 2.8 Falling Bodies
I have drawn Galileo's experiment with falling balls from the Leaning Tower of Pisa, not because he carried the experiment out there — this is disputed — but because the Leaning Tower is nice to draw. The observers were astonished — and people still are — to see approximately the same time required for different balls to fall, irrespective of their size and mass.

only did this establish the total weight of the crown, it also determined the gold/silver content. He thus introduced the principle of non-destructive testing which is so important in contemporary engineering practice.

His enquiry into natural phenomena was wide. One day, while sitting in the Basilica of Pisa, next to the Leaning Tower, he noticed a chandelier swinging gently in a draught. Irrespective of its amplitude (that is, its distance of swing), the chandelier appeared to take the same time to complete its swing, a point Galileo was able to confirm by checking with his pulse. Thus, what became known as the isochronism (the uniformity of time of swing) of pendulums was discovered and this, in the hands of Christiaan Huygens, led to the pendulum clock in 1657 when, for the first time, it became worth while to put a minute hand on a clock to exploit the resultant accuracy.

But in this period there was a further discovery that is likely to have had a major influence on the university relationships that became critical to Galileo's story. Aristotle had claimed that the speed of falling objects was a direct consequence of their weight. By a remarkable piece of inductive reasoning, Galileo showed that this could not be the case and he proved it by dropping balls of different weight from the top of a tower, popularly reckoned to be the Leaning Tower [Fig 2.8]. Further, he demonstrated the phenomenon accurately by rolling the balls down inclined planes and reproducing the effect in slow motion, 'diluting gravity', as he called it.

There were other reasons for disagreeing with Aristotle. The theory of natural motions and natural places Galileo thought to be wrong and it eventually emerged that he had, for some time, been convinced of the Copernican as opposed to the Aristotelian scheme for the heavens.

The proof with the falling balls did not make him popular. The story of the demonstration before the Professors of the University suggests a flamboyance that would not wear well in academic circles, but more important, Aristotle had been shown to be wrong — and in common with many universities of the day, Pisa was dedicated to Aristotelian thinking, both in its science and its philosophy. So unpopular did Galileo become that his colleagues would pack the back of the audiences to which he lectured to disturb him while lecturing, a habit which, I am personally glad to say, seems to have been abandoned in Pisa!

His enemies were being arrayed against him, so it was not surprising that when the three-year contract was complete, Galileo moved away and took an appointment at Padua.

It was here that the news of the invention of the telescope reached him. Excited by the prospect of a new piece of experimental equipment, Galileo had soon constructed one of his own. Its strategic importance in war was immediately obvious: enemy ships could be seen with a telescope long before they could with the unaided eye. Here was an opportunity to make money and favour, so a demonstration was arranged to point out its military advantages before his patron, the Doge of Venice. For his pains Galileo was awarded a life Chair at Padua and his salary was doubled.

Then Galileo turned his telescope upwards. Before him were

sights never before seen by man and destined to change man's concept of the universe of which he was part.

It was 1609 — and on into the next year the world was rocked by what Galileo reported. The moon's surface was found to comprise mountains and valleys rather like the earth's: it was not a 'perfect' light as Aristotle had claimed. The Milky Way was seen to be made up, not of luminous gas, but of myriads of stars that stretched across the heaven. Jupiter had four lights which rotated about it; planets that did not circulate the earth as Ptolemy had claimed they must. Then Venus was found to have phases like our moon, an observation which, with the variation in size that Galileo measured, was a clear indication that it circled the sun and not the earth, a further nail in the coffin of the earth-centred scheme for the universe. And the sun was seen to have spots.

Sunspots were perhaps the most convincing piece of evidence, but the impact was somewhat lost in the acrimonious counter-claim by a German Jesuit priest that he had discovered them and favoured the idea that they were planets circulating close to the sun's surface. Galileo had little difficulty in proving him wrong and Aristotle's other 'perfect' light was relegated along with the moon.

Aristotle and Ptolemy were shown to be wrong, Copernicus was justified in his view of a sun-centred system, and Kepler was overjoyed. But a storm was gathering for Galileo: its source was not the church, as has generally been supposed, but Galileo's erstwhile academic colleagues.

But for Galileo, the hot thrill of discovery was spurring him on as he wrote of Jupiter's moons, 'I have that faith in our blessed God that just as he showed me alone the grace of discovering so many new marvels from his hand, he will also concede to me to find the absolute order of their revolutions,' — pompous, but true, as it happened. Reporting on sunspots, he saw their use making him to be 'lifted up to the ultimate goal of our efforts, that is to the love of the Divine Artificer'.

*   *   *

Science is always wrong. It never solves a problem without raising ten more problems. Copernicus proved that Ptolemy was wrong. Kepler proved that Copernicus was wrong. Galileo proved that Aristotle was wrong. But at that point the sequence broke down, because science then came up against that incalculable phenomenon, an Englishman.

Spoken by an Englishman this would have been pure chauvinism, but it was part of a speech by George Bernard Shaw, an Irishman — and Isaac Newton was his subject. He continued:

As an Englishman, Newton was able to combine a prodigious mental faculty with the credulities and delusions that would disgrace a rabbit. As an Englishman, he postulated a rectilinear Universe because the English always use the word 'square' to denote honesty, truthfulness, in short: rectitude. Newton knew that the Universe consisted of bodies in motion, and that none of them ever moved in straight lines, or ever could. But an Englishman was not daunted by the facts. To explain why all the lines in his rectilinear Universe were bent, he invented a force called gravitation and then erected a complex British Universe and established it as a religion which was devoutly believed in for 300 years.

Newton was a phenomenon. Brought up in Grantham in England where he did little to draw attention to himself other than carve his name in the window-sill of his school-room — where it can still be seen under glass in case any other aspiring Newtons feel the urge to do the same — he went on to Cambridge to study mathematics. It was here that his brilliance flowered — and at the right time to address the problems of the new science emerging from the grip of Greek orthodoxy.

The demise of Aristotle's 'natural places' to which bodies were drawn, as well as the circulation due to his crystalline spheres which had been a convenience to Ptolemy and had influenced Copernicus, had left a problem. What kept the planets moving and orbiting around the sun without visible means of support or locomotion?

Kepler had concluded that, since the planets revolved around the sun, there was a sun-centred force acting upon them and this he presumed to be magnetic. Galileo disagreed. It was ludicrous, he said, to imagine forces reaching through space grasping at bodies so that, for instance, the tides on the earth could be affected by the moon.

Newton had already sharpened his intellect on other physical problems. He had split light into its constituent rainbow colours by

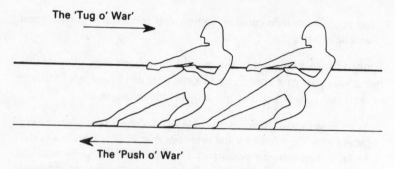

Fig 2.9 The Tug o' War Team

It doesn't matter how strong the tug o' war team is, if their feet slip, then they are likely to lose the match. Newtonian theory says that they can only pull on the rope to the same extent as they can push with their feet.

passing it through a prism and reunited it as white light by passing it through another. He had discovered the binomial theorem, an important tool for mathematical calculations, and he had invented his 'method of fluxions', the calculus, the most powerful and far-reaching weapon that mathematicians and scientists have ever handled. He had also invented a new type of telescope, of which the one through which I first saw Saturn was a copy. So far-reaching were his interests that, eventually, scientific thinking in general was formed upon his foundations.

Now he was addressing the problems of the movement of heavenly bodies, wondering why the moon kept its path around the earth. The story of the falling apple may be apocryphal, in the same mould as Galileo and the Leaning Tower, but it certainly came as an inspiration to him that all objects were attracted to all other objects. Spurred by a barbed relationship with Robert Hooke, who was also working along the same lines, Newton finally emerged from his isolation with the universal law of gravity. Every object in the universe exerted an attractive force on every other object and therefore contributed to its motion. Thus, as the apple fell towards the earth, so too did the earth towards the apple. This attractive force varied, not as the distance separating the objects, but as the distance squared (that is, multiplied by itself). Thus, as the separation between the planets grew, the force they exerted upon one another fell very rapidly.

Force and motion were central to Newton's thinking. He

concluded that every force had an equal and opposite force in attendance. The tug-o'-war team can only exert a pull on the rope so long as its feet are firmly fixed on the ground, pushing in the opposite direction [Fig 2.9]. An object did not have speed because of an applied force: rather, its speed was maintained because there was no applied force. A space probe travelling to the moon does not operate its engines continuously. Having left the gravitational pull of the earth and in the absence of wind resistance, it continues to travel with the same speed and in the same direction until the influence of the moon's gravity is great enough or its engines are switched on. When this happens, its speed or its direction, or both, change. The object accelerates or decelerates because of a force applied. A china ornament dropped from a great height is almost certain to break, whereas that which just topples over may not. The tendency to shatter is directly related to the speed at which the ornament hits the ground and this is controlled by the height from which it falls. During the time that it is falling, it is under the influence of gravitational force which accelerates it continuously.

Newton's laws of motion, as they were known, flatly contradicted earlier understanding of force and motion. The Aristotelian framework made the presence of force necessary to maintain constant speed. The Newtonian system made the absence of force the vital predicate to maintain constant speed. For Aristotle, force resulted in speed. For Newton, force resulted in acceleration, the rate of change of speed.

Isaac Newton thus perceived that the movement of heavenly bodies, the planets for example, was governed by a force system dictated by a few simple and elegant mathematical statements. With no external force to affect it, the earth would hurtle through space in an unerring straight line, leaving behind familiar objects like the members of the planetary system it knew, which themselves went in their own direction. Because of the sun's massive presence, however, the earth and other planets moved in a gravitational field whose attractive forces pulled them towards it. This centripetal force (radially inward towards the sun) was at exactly the level to bend the linear flight of the earth and the planets into a curve that was the closed ellipse Kepler had discovered. The speed at which the earth followed its trajectory varied as its position relative to the sun, according to Newton's laws, and his predictions happened to be exactly in harmony with Kepler's conclusions of a constant area swept in a set time period by the line from the earth to the sun.

Newton's system of mechanics controlled the universe!

In writing his explanation of this momentous discovery, Newton concluded, 'This most beautiful system of the sun, planets, and comets, could only proceed from the council and dominion of an intelligent and powerful Being [who] governs all things ... and on account of his dominion he is wont to be called Lord God.' In his investigations, Newton saw a 'God of order, not confusion'.

Newton realised that, universal in application as his laws were, they still only explained the *how* of the cosmos, nothing more. 'The cause of gravity I do not know.' He knew *how* gravity operated — he did not know *why* it did. Nevertheless, Newton's laws were a detailed explanation of a mechanical universe, the vast celestial clockwork. The position of Mars and all the planets was now accurately predicted — that is, except Mercury, which somehow didn't quite fit. Mercury had replaced Mars as the astronomers' conundrum.

CHAPTER THREE

COSMOS REVIEWED: A PATH FROM DETERMINISM

THE IDEA THAT THE COSMOS is a deterministic system, mechanical in its operation and predictable in its behaviour, is attractive. It deals with many uncertainties, assuring us of the future as well as the past. Aristotle's scheme — a series of concentric spheres sliding across one another in an ordered fashion, appealed to this sense of mechanism. Kepler, because he had solved the problem of the planetary paths, had proved repeatability, a sign of the mechanistic universe. From the sidelines, Pierre Laplace the French mathematician had put it this way: 'All the effects of nature are only the mathematical consequence of a small number of immutable laws.' In other words, everything is eventually governed by a set of unchanging rules — and there aren't many of them.

Newton had finally put shape to this mechanism. Every action had a reaction: acceleration of an object, whether an apple or a planet, was directly related to its mass and the force applied to it. In the absence of a force to create an acceleration, objects would continue precisely as they were — the stationary would stay stationary, the moving would continue to move as they had done, both in direction and speed. His prescription of the laws of motion and the universal law of gravity said it all, and these were eventually understood to describe a mechanistic universe which left nothing for the Galileo's Divine Artificer to do. He could join the queues of the unemployed.

Had the question been asked, 'Is the end in sight for theoretical physics?', the answer would have been an unequivocal yes. Everything was in place and matched, except the disagreeable behaviour of Mercury.

But the hope that physics already had all the answers was dashed by an apparently insignificant observation. In Denmark, the needle of a compass was seen to move when placed near a wire carrying an electrical charge. Magnetism and electricity had been known about for some while — magnetism since 600 BC — yet no relationship between them had ever been considered. The moving needle changed all that, becoming the trigger for a revolution in physics, cosmology and the lifestyle of civilisation.

News of the moving needle came to London and to Michael Faraday at the Royal Institution which he had joined as an assistant in 1813. Self-taught, apprenticed to a bookseller and trained as a book-binder, he had developed a consuming interest in science which had led him to the Royal Institution where, by 1821, he carried the grand title of 'Assistant and Superintendent of the Apparatus of the Laboratory and Mineralogical Collection'.

Faraday was an experimenter — he has sometimes been called our greatest experimental philosopher. His interest in electricity had begun when, as a book-binder, he had the job of rebinding a worn copy of the 'E' to 'F' section of *Encyclopedia Britannica*, and read, over and over again, the article on electricity. He was soon able therefore to reproduce the experiment with the moving needle, which he did in 1821. But it was a further ten years before the results of his enquiring mind produced the picture that began to assault the Newtonian scheme of things.

By moving a magnet through a loop of wire, Faraday found that a current was created in the wire. This is accepted without question by today's schoolchildren, as is the discovery of lines of magnetic force by pouring iron filings on to a card placed above a magnet. But for Faraday, it posed a problem. How did the current occur? His answer involved introducing the concept of a field surrounding the magnet. We understand fields to be filled with grass but this field was permeated by lines of magnetic force, as we can see with the iron filings. Yet the break-through for Faraday came as he realised that the current was not a result of the wire being in the field of magnetic force, rather in passing through the field — either a moving wire loop or a moving magnetic field was essential to create a current.

This has become central to the comfort of our homes and work. The computer on which I am typing this manuscript — the electric light which may be helping you to read this book — the refrigerator that keeps your food fresh and, in all likelihood, the cooker that will be used in the preparation of your next meal, all depend upon it, for this is the principle of the electrical generator whose power you use.

But Faraday went further: he made the extraordinary suggestion that the electrical and magnetic forces in this demonstration did not transmit instantaneously, they took time. This astonishing idea contradicted Newton whose laws could not accommodate it. The further proposition that force did not emanate from a point but was contained in a field also offended the Newtonian picture.

It was such insight that brought fame to Faraday. In summing up this remarkable life, the secretary of the Royal Institution said, 'His standard of duty was ... not founded upon any intuitive ideas of right and wrong, nor was it fashioned upon any outward experiences of time and place, but it was formed entirely on what he held to be the revelation of God in the written word.' He certainly believed that 'the book of nature, which we have to read, is written by the finger of God'. This was no abstract, compartmentalised view. His assistant Tyndall reported, 'His religious feeling and his philosophy could not be kept apart: there was an habitual overflow of the one into the other.'

His laboratory in the Royal Institution was visited by the famous and the influential. On one occasion, the British Chancellor of the Exchequer — finance and tax controller for the nation — went to the Royal Institution laboratory. Seeing an experiment in electricity he asked,

'But Faraday, my dear fellow, what's the use of it?'

'Why, there is every probability that you will soon be able to tax it,' was the prophetic reply.

By the time of his death in 1867, Faraday had been awarded unsolicited honours from ninety-seven international academies of science. It remained, though, for his observations on the intimate relationship between magnetism and electricity to be set down in formal mathematical terms. This was the task of James Clerk-Maxwell.

Like Faraday, Clerk-Maxwell was a man of wide-ranging interests. He first leapt to fame in 1855 when, at the age of twenty-four, he won a prize at Cambridge for a study on the rings of

Saturn. His prediction that they comprised a cloud of well-ordered small bodies wasn't confirmed until one hundred and twenty-five years later with the flight of the American space shot, Voyager. He made other significant contributions in science — but he is best known for the advances on Faraday's work. Not only did he formalise the observations made in the laboratory of the Royal Institution, he added significantly to them. He saw that, just as a current resulted from a change in a magnetic field, so also a magnetic field was altered by a change in current; each responded to the other and were parts of a unified electromagnetic field. The manner in which Clerk-Maxwell discovered this two-way relationship appeals to the artist in us all. Having established the equations governing both the magnetic and electric fields, he found that they lacked balance. Responding to his aesthetic sense, he added a term to obtain the balance in appearance, only to find that, while he had been considering the production of an electric field by varying a magnetic field, the added term accounted for the production of a magnetic field by varying an electric field. Symmetry in the equations was the means of making a fundamental discovery. Further, since it took time for each field to respond to the other, Clerk-Maxwell saw these changes taking the form of waves which, he concluded, moved at the speed of light.

This highlighted the essential difference from Newton's view. It is this. If by a remarkable piece of cosmic skullduggery, the sun was to be removed instantly and without trace we would know about it immediately, according to Newton. Clerk-Maxwell concluded, however, that the catastrophic news would be sent to us at the speed of light, reaching us about eight minutes after the event [Fig 3.1]. Not that this would make a great deal of difference to us. The eight minutes elapsed time would not allow us to set things in order for the event, for there would be no way of knowing that it had happened other than by a message which, itself, was travelling at the speed of light and therefore reaching us at the same time as the effect of losing a sun to revolve around.

But it did make a great deal of difference to the development of theoretical physics. In showing that, being constrained to the finite speed of light, communication could not take place instantaneously, Clerk-Maxwell had demonstrated the incomplete nature of Newton's mechanics and set the stage for something

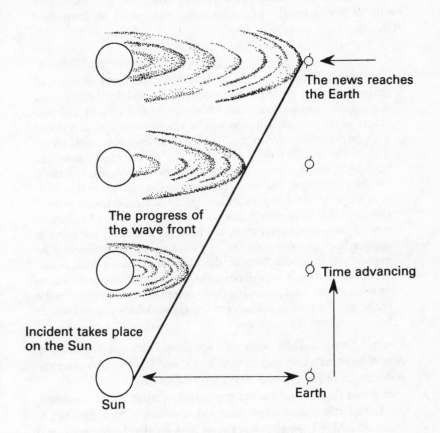

The news reaches
the Earth

The progress of
the wave front

Time advancing

Incident takes place
on the Sun

Earth

Sun

Fig 3.1 Travelling News

Time advances in this figure as the eye moves up the page past the four sets of drawings of the sun and earth. An incident at the sun's surface in the bottom picture radiates news in a wave which reached the earth about eight minutes later in the top picture. This shows the difference between Clerk-Maxwell and Newton whose mechanics indicated that the message would be transmitted instantaneously.

new. Einstein viewed it this way, 'The formulation of these equations is the most important event in physics since Newton's time, not only because of their wealth of content but also because they form a pattern for a new type of law.' That new type of law came into being and with it, a form of physics taking the observer even further from the common-sense pattern of Ptolemy and Aristotle.

*   *   *

Three hundred years after its establishment [the theory of universal gravity], a young professor rises calmly in the middle of Europe and says to our astronomers, 'Gentlemen: if you will observe the next eclipse of the sun carefully, you will be able to explain what is wrong with the perihelion of Mercury.' The civilised Newtonian world replies that, if the dreadful thing is true, if the eclipse makes good the blasphemy, the next thing the young professor will do is to question the existence of gravity. The young professor smiles and says that gravitation is a very useful hypothesis and gives fairly good results in most cases, but that he personally can do without it. He is asked to explain how, if there is no gravitation, the heavenly bodies do not move in straight lines and run clear out of the Universe. He replies that no explanation is needed because the Universe is not rectilinear and exclusively British; it is curvilinear. The Newtonian Universe thereupon drops dead and is supplanted by the Einstein Universe. Einstein has not challenged the facts of science, but the axioms of science, and science has surrendered the challenge.

George Bernard Shaw was still speaking. He was introducing Albert Einstein to an audience in 1930, just fifteen years after the publication of his General Theory of Relativity.

It was a theory that rocked the world, tearing away, it seemed, the last of any reason in physics and cosmology. Straight lines in space no longer existed, funny things happened at high speeds, and time was a variable that could advance at different rates. Nothing was now fixed — and it was all because Faraday and Clerk-Maxwell had the idea that messages took time to get from one place to another.

Einstein had posed the question, 'If my image travels at the speed of light and I am in a spaceship which itself is travelling at the speed of light, will I see a reflection of myself in a mirror held ahead of me in the direction in which I am moving?' It was a facile question yet, lurking just beneath the surface were problems whose solutions led to the laws of physics being rewritten. Einstein knew that if the mirror held in his hand was travelling at the same speed as the light waves comprising his image, they would never reach the mirror to be reflected from the surface. But he knew that was a wrong conclusion since, from the time of Newton, it had been recognised that we have no sensation of speed, only of acceleration. Thus, in the absence of an outside point of reference — a view of the road we are travelling along or a measurement on a speedometer which is connected to the road by the rotation of the road-wheels — we can never know anything about our speed. So if he could not see his reflection in the mirror, he would know the speed at which he was travelling, that of light. But that was impossible without an external point of reference. If, however, there was a reflection, as he was able to convince himself, then the light waves must travel at a speed greater than the speed of light — but that was also impossible.

It is reported that, pondering this, he occasionally thought he was going mad!

Eventually questioning the validity of all the factors involved, he reached several conclusions. At speeds close to that of light, time slows down — a clock would actually tick less quickly. In addition, at such speeds the dimension of an object in the direction of travel is reduced. A train, the example he had in mind, would actually get shorter. In case weight-conscious people think that this may be the answer to their slimming problems, a further consequence was also noted by Einstein. Since nothing could travel faster than the speed of light, the mass of an object necessarily increased with speed, reaching an infinite value at the speed of light! Thus it would require an infinite force, which in any case is unattainable, to accelerate an infinite mass beyond the speed of light.

From these fundamental conclusions there grew a new concept of the universe — no longer space in the three-dimensional sense that we think of and time as an independent quantity which varies uniformly everywhere always — but a system of 'spacetime' which is curved by the mass of the planets, stars and other objects in it.

The concept of curved spacetime is so far beyond our normal grasp that it is best described by analogy. Consider a trampoline as it is found in a gymnasium. The surface is normally stretched taut and therefore flat — and this represents to us the surface of

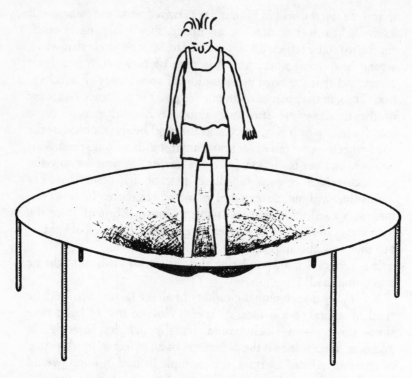

Fig 3.2 The Trampoline
The weight of the gymnast standing on the trampoline distorts its surface so that there are dents where his feet rest. The curvature of the surface is greatest at his feet and diminishingly small further away. This is analogous to Einstein's understanding of space-warp — replacing gravity — due to the mass of objects like planets. See fig 3.3

spacetime. When a person stands on the trampoline, the surface is distorted and the region around is curved to accommodate his weight where his feet stand [Fig 3.2]. If others join him on the trampoline, similar deformations occur at different places on the surface. These represent the effect of masses like the sun, the earth and so on upon the spacetime surface of the universe: the mass creates the curvature [Fig 3.3].

Einstein had now left behind everything that appealed to common sense — reason and intuition had no harmony with such weird ideas. To say that seeing is believing had become meaningless. Yet even if we dismiss Einstein's ideas because they don't

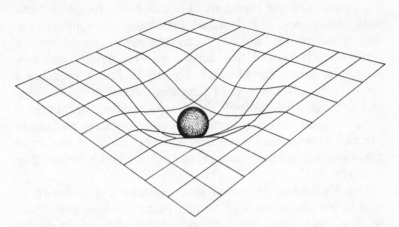

Fig 3.3 Space Warp
Replacing the gymnast's feet on the trampoline (fig 3.2) with a planet supported on an elastic sheet representing space, we have a picture like this. Of course, the surface portrayed is two-dimensional whereas space is three-dimensional.

appeal to our sense of the reasonable, George Bernard Shaw was right — applying them to the path of Mercury got rid of the error measured when using the Newtonian equations — almost! Einstein's principles worked.

*   *   *

Twentieth-century advances in physics have been weighty with ideas that don't seem to be reasonable. Specifically, particle physics, the physics of the very, very small which it is generally reckoned holds the key to the questions dominating cosmology and cosmogony, the physics of the very, very large, have produced concepts that are breathtaking in their oddity.

Just after the turn of the century, Max Planck produced the quantum theory. In this he claimed that energy transmission wasn't continuously variable in strength — as we can vary in a continuous manner the volume of a radio set — but that it was packaged in small blocks known as quanta.

This was a fundamental break with classical physics because the deterministic world of cause and effect of which Laplace had dreamed and to which Newton had contributed, began to break down in the observer's eyes. Newton had been concerned with the large world and the behaviour of bodies as we recognise them, stars, planets, objects that moved. Planck was more interested in the microscopic world, the atom, its constituents and sub-species. Newton had declared that actions had reactions, there were identifiable causes for all observable effects. Planck produced a gaming table of chance: everything was reduced to a probability and although it was possible therefore to make statistical predictions of great accuracy, simply because so many myriads of particles were engaged in any action, the behaviour of *any one* of the attendant particles was a matter of chance rather than certainty.

Planck's thinking arose from his consideration of the behaviour of a single photon of light (a light particle) whose energy was reckoned not to be freely divisible but comprised irreducible packets which he called quanta. In conservative language, on the occasion at which he received the Nobel Prize for his work, Planck said of the quantum theory that it was either 'a fictitious magnitude . . . more or less an illusion . . . a game with formulae, or the deduction of the law is based upon a true physical idea'. Evidence accumulated over the years pointed to the latter.

The years also produced some strange elaborations of which the oddest is possibly the uncertainty principle proposed by Heisenberg. He said that it is impossible to assign to a particle both its position in space and its motion at the same time. But if bodies comprise particles and their energy is expressed in motion — their temperature is a measure of energy — how can we say that we don't know where they are? Further, it is impossible to say by which path a particle travels from one point to another — it has a large number of possible routes from which to choose and it is even suggested that it doesn't take one of them; it takes all of them!

Then there is the question of atoms. Niels Bohr suggested that the atom is a nebulous will o' the wisp until it is isolated in an observation: only then does it become real, but its reality is restricted to a knowledge of its position *or* its motion, never both. If an atom is not there until we look for it, how certain can I be that the desk at which I sit writing this — made of wood, comprising molecules made up of atoms — is there? Or how can I be certain that I — also constructed of molecules and atoms — am here? In the Institute for Theoretical Physics at the University of

California in Santa Barbara, the faculty members have liberally used newspaper cartoons as wall coverings to dispel the seriousness of their profound thoughts. On one door is a drawing of a man — evidently from his tousled hair and baggy suit he is a research nuclear physicist, a reincarnation of an Einstein — standing in front of a blackboard covered in suitable mathematics, looking in astonishment and horror from the page of the cartoon, saying, 'Good heavens, I've just proved I don't exist!'

But what is the atom? It was originally given this name, coined from the Greek word which means 'that which cannot be divided', because that is precisely what it was assumed to be — an indivisible entity which was the basic building-brick of the universe. Then the atom was split and sub-atomic particles were discovered. What then is the smallest particle — the basic element of structure? Leptons, quarks, electrons, muons, tau-neutrinos, photons, gravitons and gluons are species or sub-species that, with others, elbow one another in this sub-atomic world. Can there be more, even smaller? Or is there a smallest, that is indivisible, particle? Perhaps sub-division can continue for ever. Maybe the jingle, 'Big fleas have little fleas upon their backs to bite 'em, little fleas have smaller fleas and so *ad infinitum*,' has a stronger scientific content than suspected.

Then there is the question of the structure of light. What is it? Light particles are without mass — otherwise, according to Einstein, they couldn't travel at the speed of light, when their mass would be infinite! The corpuscular nature of light was established by Newton and light rays behaved well in accordance with Newtonian laws: they went in straight lines, they reflected from a surface, they refracted in passing between air and water, just as Newton's laws required. Known as photons in today's science, it is also now known that they don't always behave as particles. Light sometimes has the characteristics of waves, quite different from particles. This results in a scientific fudge which we call the particle/wave duality, in which light sometimes is ascribed with the behaviour of a stream of particles and sometimes that of waves. This can lead to strange conclusions. A standard laboratory experiment which happens to have application in scientific measurements of a non-intrusive nature, for example visual measurements in very high speed flow of air, is that of a light source like an electric light bulb, through a pair of slits. A screen placed beyond the slits shows an alternating set of bands of light and shade. These are called interference fringes. They result from the waves through the two slits alternately reinforcing and cancelling each other out. They lead us to the conclusion that, from the corpuscular point of view, a particle of light travels through, not one, but both slits at the same time!

Are the ideas of quantum theory, uncertainty principles and relativity taking us to the nirvana of the fulfilment of all physics, a complete understanding of the cosmos? Is the end of theoretical physics in sight? The understandable, material and deterministic world is crumbling before our eyes. It is being replaced by something amorphous, more clouded with questions than illuminated with answers. The certainty of Newton has been replaced by the uncertainty of Bohr and Heisenberg.

But does this mean that, because we don't understand it and it isn't resonant with our common sense, it is nonsense? The proof of its value eventually is whether it works. The Ptolemaic system didn't quite work out, neither did the Newtonian system. Do quantum mechanics and uncertainty principles work and, to recall the question of the Chancellor of the Exchequer, do they have any use? Paul Davies answers that by example in *God and the New Physics*.

> The image in a television screen is produced by myriads of light pulses emitted when electrons fired from a gun at the back of the set strike the fluorescent screen. The picture you perceive is reasonably sharp because the number of electrons involved is enormous, and by the law of averages, the cumulative effect of many electrons is predictable. However, any particular electron, with its inbuilt unpredictability, could go anywhere on the screen. The arrival of this electron at a place, and the fragment of the picture it produces, is uncertain. According to Bohr's philosophy bullets from an ordinary gun follow a precise path to their target, but electrons from an electron gun simply turn up at the target. And however good your aim, no bull's eye is guaranteed.

So, although we don't know *how*, we do know that the television set works.

And of relativity, we can say that Mercury's path can now be predicted — almost.

The rather neat concept of a world of deterministic mechanics has evaporated in this century, cause and effect having given way to probabilities. Effects no longer seem to have causes — at least causes that we can quantify in scientific terms. This prompted one of Einstein's most famous remarks, recorded when he was faced with the quantum theory to which he took some exception, 'God does not play dice.' Although we may not be able to see the cause because of the maelstrom of atomic activity, beneath our observations there is a deeper level of description, in Einstein's opinion. Einstein may have been right, but the deeper level may be one that goes beyond the universe's measurable physics whose answers are displayed on instrument dials or as computer output.

Quantum theory has redirected our gaze from the mechanistic world of cause and effect towards one in which effects do not appear to have causes as we can or ever will be able to measure them. There is an unknown factor beyond the scientist's instruments. Einstein would concur at this point, certainly in the matter of our current ability to probe the deeper level. What twentieth-century physics is bringing us to, however, is a recognition that the *how* can take us from the world of galaxies into that of particle physics, but it brings us to a place where the clearly defined mechanisms of precision no longer hold — and the *why* therefore remains beyond our grasp.

Rather like the fractal pictures we shall mention later, science seems to be a subject that, the further you look into, the more there is to discover and the end may never be reached in the scientist's search for the *why*. Hamlet may, after all, have been right: 'There are more things in heaven and earth, Horatio, than are dreamt of in your philosophy.'

CHAPTER FOUR

FROM ORDER TO DISORDER

RECOGNITION THAT THE COSMOS was a dynamic thing, changing in shape, structure and content, had led science away from the Aristotelian idea of a fixed, immovable firmament. Brahe's supernova was the means of unlocking a new dimension in considering the universe. (Admittedly Chinese observers had witnessed the supernova in the Crab nebula in AD 1054, but the significance of this event was not yet appreciated.) So far as our eyes could discern, things may have been happening very slowly, but the universe was changing. The remains of the supernova of Brahe can still be seen. No longer a brilliant light in the constellation of Cassiopeia, the debris of the explosion is recognised, over 400 years later, as a cloud of gas dispersing from the point of the original light source. In due course, it would be recognised that processes — changes — abounded in the universe and those that kept it in a ferment of activity were, like all others, described by thermodynamic criteria.

Yet the origins of thermodynamics were not in a starry vault or on the page of elegant mathematics describing some piece of theoretical physics. They were rooted in the prosaic surroundings of eighteenth-century engineering workshops and embraced a brewery as well as the desire to see a war won. And they depended upon one thing above all else: an understanding of what fire was.

The primitive idea of the alchemist was that like earth, water and air, fire was an element. Gigantic intellectual leaps were necessary to take man's understanding of energy from this to the more refined views expressed in the two laws of thermodynamics. These laws make two simple but profound declarations. The first is that in a system, which in our case we might define as the universe,

60

the total amount of energy in existence always remains constant. Its form may change, as we shall see, but it is a fundamental constraint upon nature that energy can be neither created nor destroyed: it merely changes its form in any process. The second is that all processes are wasteful to some degree. Of the energy available for a stipulated task, some is squandered. This is not finally dependent upon our efficiency in doing a particular job, but is in the nature of things. That waste of energy, which can no longer be usefully employed, is measured as an increase in a quantity called entropy, a form of useless energy. These laws are all-inclusive, fundamental, their legislation reaching into every part of life and area of the scientist's investigation. The leaps necessary to get us to an understanding of these thermodynamic laws take us via waterwheels to the Napoleonic war in 1815. We pass through the workshop of a brewery and on to the unlikely environment of the steam engine, the direct ancestor of the fairground engine that still occasionally operates the fairground carousels, making much fuss about it.

But the story does not stop there. Fundamental rules have universal application. The main difference between a steam engine and the normal car engine is simply that in one, fuel is burned outside, and in the other, inside the cylinder. The principle difference between the car engine and the gas turbine is that fuel is burned intermittently in one and continuously in the other, a series of bangs as opposed to a roar. Although shapes are different, the operation is similar for all of them and the descriptive rules are the same.

But universality leads to interdependence between scientific fields. The rules used in designing an office block also apply to a tree standing in a gale: if both fall down it will, in all likelihood, be because the same rules have been broken in each instance. And the life processes of the tree are accurately maintained within the same laws of thermodynamics that govern engines. The effect of the laws of thermodynamics was eventually recognised to be all-embracing, describing every process known to man, from the germination of a seed to a nuclear reaction. Our sun was seen to operate according to them, as did every other sun, that is, every star in the universe.

Thermodynamics is a form of accountancy, like the management of a family income. The head of the house controls the money, allowing for taxes, food, domestic costs, vehicle expenses and savings for the holiday, balancing these against the family's total income. The thermodynamicist does exactly the same for energy, using two instruments known as the two laws of thermodynamics.

The First Law balances the energy in a system — that is the simple book-keeping exercise. The Second Law says that some of the energy in a system must be forfeited, leaving in consequence only a part for useful employment. This is rather like the Inland Revenue saying that some of a person's income must be taxed. How much is calculated from the tax laws and usually depends on the circumstances of the individual. Similarly, how much energy is forfeited in a process, depends upon the process — the individual circumstances. The thermodynamicist is the engineering tax-man, dictating what the laws demand and, rather like the tax-man (the engineer will tell you) he does so without becoming personally rich in the process!

*   *   *

Having considered that fire was one of four elements, it was an enormous step to view it differently, as the mark of a particular type of chemical process. But when it was recognised that this produced heat which could be usefully employed and measured, thermodynamics was born.

It remained to be established that heat was itself not a thing like water which could pass through a watermill, providing power, but still remaining water.

James Joule was the son of a wealthy English brewer. With the profits made from the Englishman's habit of drinking beer and using his father's company workshops, the inquisitive Joule began to study heat. During the period of 1840 to 1850, his experiments showed that it was not conserved. The analogy of water gushing through a waterwheel was incorrect! Joule's discovery hinged upon the observation that heat could be changed into work — this happens in a car engine. The process could also be reversed: work could be changed into heat — this happens in a car's brakes. That one was the equivalent of the other gave birth to the unit of heat, the Joule, named after James himself.

We can check that James Joule was right on the exchange of work and heat merely by rubbing our hands together. The warmth we feel is a consequence of the work done, that is, the effort made in moving the hands.

In due course, other forms of energy were added to the list of equivalents. The parallel to the domestic accountant is that his money could be reckoned in different forms, house, furniture, cash, bank account and so on. The different expressions of energy and their interchangeability eventually led to the First Law of thermodynamics, a simple accounting of energy, making it constant in a particular system, no matter how small or large, an engine or the universe.

*   *   *

Sadi Carnot was French, and like his family, a republican and a patriot. His father was a mathematician who had attended the École Militaire in Paris. Because he was not of aristocratic stock, the saying at the École, 'the competent were not noble and the noble were not competent', probably enhanced his republicanism, faithfully reproduced in his son.

Sadi was intellectually strong and grounded in mathematics. He had seen the demise of the French fighting-force in the Napoleonic wars: no match eventually for the British fighting-machine or for the rigours of the march on Moscow, the army faced disaster. How could the cause of France be best supported?

He recognised that the superior weapons needed for success in war were the product of better manufacturing industry. This, he determined, was a consequence of the Industrial Revolution which, since 1776, had depended increasingly upon the steam engine to drive it. Because of the work of British engineers, Newcomen, Trevithick, Watt and Boulton, the British had steam engines of enviable design and quality. They could be used in mines, for which the steam engine had largely been developed, producing the fuel and material of industry. They could move industrial products efficiently. Sadi Carnot concluded that whoever had the best steam engines could conquer the world. The better they were understood, the better they could be made to work.

To understand that this quality of British steam engines was measured by a different standard from today's, we should over-hear James Watt enthusing over his machine, noting that he could only just push a worn shilling (today's five pence piece, or an American quarter dollar) between the piston and the cylinder!

Sadi Carnot established the unlikely and staggering principle, which he published in 1824, that for the steam engine to use its available energy, some had to be thrown away.

We can picture Sadi's discovery in this manner. High energy steam in the cylinder did work which could be used. However, before more high energy steam could repeat the process, the steam which had already done its job had to be got out of the cylinder. But that steam still contained some energy. Thus, while most of the energy drove the engine, some went, with the used steam, into the exhaust. That energy could not be recovered: it was lost to the atmosphere. [Fig 4.1]

Unknowingly, Sadi Carnot had established a fundamental feature of all processes: nature has a dissymmetry which declares that in any process, some energy will be wasted. And if it is wasted, then it cannot be reused in that particular process. In a real situation, then, the process can never return to its starting point with its original allocation of heat intact and available for use.

Now that is an intellectually profound discovery — we call it irreversibility — which today is accepted without question. We know that the exhaust from a car engine is hot, indicating that it is taking energy from the engine, just as we know that the engine must be cooled and this also takes energy away from it. These heat losses are signs of this irreversibility. Without the use of a heat pump — a kind of refrigerator in reverse — we cannot regain from the atmosphere the heat lost to it. Even the use of a heat pump involves irreversible losses of heat to the atmosphere. The irreversible loss of heat is a sign that the process from which the heat came must have been irreversible. We cannot make the process go backwards.

But this dissymmetry is also demonstrated in other everyday events. A piece of china may fall from a table and break into pieces but, much as we would like it to, the reverse does not happen. Potteries are profitable businesses as a result. Rivers flow downhill: none is known that actually flows back up a hill. It remains for the process of weather, wind and rain to return the water to the hilltop

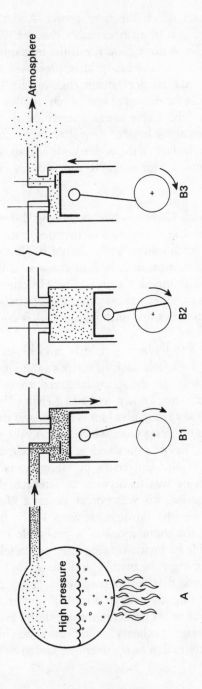

Fig 4.1 The Steam Engine

Water is boiled at high pressure in the boiler at A and the steam is fed to the steam engine cylinder at B1. The piston is pushed down the cylinder by the high pressure, rotating the crankshaft to produce power. In reaching the bottom of the piston stroke at B2, the steam pressure in the cylinder is lowered by expansion. The low-pressure steam must be ejected before more steam can enter the cylinder and this is done by the crankshaft pushing the piston back up the cylinder (B3) to expel the steam to atmosphere. The energy released to the atmosphere contributes to an increase in entropy.

and the spring from which the river grows. And that process involves the use of heat in an irreversible manner. We may not recognise them to be so immediately, but the breaking china and the flowing river are both thermodynamic processes.

In his pursuit of the efficient steam engine, Sadi Carnot was establishing the most fundamental law of nature. But he was not to know this. Yet the implications gained from the gasping leviathans, operating at the head of deep shaft mines and threatening to change both the face of the countryside and society, were to be profound. It remained for others to run with Carnot's ideas.

*   *   *

James Joule and Sadi Carnot, while examining different aspects of what was to become the science of thermodynamics, were in contradiction with each other. While Carnot had established the inevitability of loss in a process, he had considered that he was working with an unchangeable commodity. He called it caloric. Joule, on the other hand, had shown that this commodity, which he identified as heat, was not unchangeable — it could become work.

It was feared that if Joule was right — and his evidence was impressive — then the whole basis of Carnot's thinking would be undermined. This was the thought that taxed another scientist, William Thompson, later known as Lord Kelvin. The name by which history generally recognises him is Kelvin and this has been lent to the temperature scale most widely used in the world.

At the age of ten, Kelvin's outstanding academic qualities were evident: he went to the University of Glasgow as an undergraduate. Although he was to become an intellectual giant and outstanding theoretician, his was not an abstract life. He made money, becoming wealthy through his work in the field of telegraphy and laying the foundations of a profitable industry still given to his ideas. He had wide-ranging interests. In telegraphy he was, among other things, the man behind the laying of the trans-Atlantic cable. It is said that he proposed marriage using the signalling lamp from the ship involved in a cable-laying exercise to the chosen lady who was at her home on the sea-shore! He worked in the field of electro-magnetic theory. So important was his contribution to thermodynamics that he is sometimes said to be its founder.

For four years Kelvin grappled with the problem of the apparent differences between Carnot and Joule, viewing the subject in a basic, yet global manner. By 1851 he was drawn to the tentative conclusion that nature responded, not to one global law as had been thought, but to two. These operated in parallel, each demanding obedience at all times, but each making its own separate statement about the use of heat. One dealt with energy in its various forms, the book-keeping of which we have spoken. We now know this as the First Law and it dealt the death blow to caloric. In addition, acknowledging the dissymmetry in the processes of nature which Carnot had discovered, the Second Law declared a tax on the available energy, making processes irreversible.

Although these laws had yet to be put into a working shape that would make them the vital tools they are to the scientist, the realisation that nature is described ultimately by two laws, not one, must count as the critical step in the development of thermo-dynamics at the hands of these intellectual giants. This is possibly the most profound and sweeping discovery made in the history of science.

*   *   *

Carnot had discovered the principle of irreversibility; Joule had found that energy could exist in different equivalent forms; Kelvin had put their thoughts together and discovered that processes were governed by two parallel universal laws. To put these laws into a manageable form that could be used by scientists, it was necessary to change the perspective on the processes from global to detailed.

In a steam engine, Carnot had determined, some of the energy had been channelled into useful work for which the engine had been designed, a coherent action. The remainder had gone along a different route — out of the exhaust — to heat up the atmosphere, an incoherent action. This matter of coherence and incoherence has an analogy in a windy day. In the open air, the direction of the wind is easily felt — it is coherent — but behind an obstruction, like a wall, the wind which is clearly still there and whose effect may be seen in leaves scurrying about, often does not seem to have any directional preference. It is random and chaotic; incoherent.

It was this random, chaotic effect, examined at a microscopic level, that grasped the interest of Rudolph Clausius. Born only ten years before Carnot's death in 1832, Clausius was in the vanguard of scientific thinking built upon the foundations of Carnot. Clausius was still in his twenties when he recognised that the amount of randomness, or increase of chaos, represented the inefficiency of the system — he called it entropy. He concluded that in any real process, that is one in which there is irreversibility, the entropy increased. His formulation of the Second Law states the inevitability of the increase in entropy in any process. It doesn't matter how small or large it is. While Carnot's object of interest was a steam engine, the object could be as big as a power station or it could include both the power station and countryside around it: there is no size limit, in which case we can speak of a process bounding the universe.

Now the operation of the universe involves processes. At the microscopic level, the multiplication of cells, or in the largest frame of reference, the light emanating from galaxies as their suns burn out, are all processes — progression from one state to another. Every process is ultimately thermodynamic and it is irreversible. It must therefore involve an increase of entropy. Adding together the entropy rise from all the sources in the universe is an impossible feat, but it requires no stretch of the imagination to understand that, large as it is, with so many contributory forces, the universe's entropy is remorselessly increasing. In fact, we can say that all natural processes are accompanied by an increase of entropy in the universe and since entropy is increasing, the level of chaos in the universe must necessarily be increasing also.

The thoughtless and autocratic demand of the two thermo-dynamic laws that they should be obeyed at all times has been the cause of many failed inventions, in particular of perpetual motion machines. A perpetual motion machine violates the laws of thermodynamics and, attractive as it looks on paper, it can never work. I was asked by a hopeful inventor to appraise his solution for the energy problems of the world which, in passing, would make for very cheap motoring. His design, for which he had obtained patent papers, involved a windmill set on the roof of a car. The car accelerated from a stationary position, using its engine as normal. At an appropriate speed, when the windmill was revolving fast enough because of the speed of the car, an ingenious gearbox shifted the power drive from the engine, which was then switched off, to the windmill which took over driving the car. The enviable efficiency of this device was enhanced by putting the windmill in a duct with a bellmouth to encourage more air through its blades to supercharge it. The only problem seemed to be how to fit brakes powerful enough to stop the car in view of the surging power that resulted. Sadly, another problem lurked just beneath the surface: power was coming out but no energy was going in — the tell-tale evidence of a perpetual motion machine. He lost his investment. But so too did a friend who, less than a year before this was written, saw a different form of perpetual motion machine advertised on American television, inviting subscription for equity in the manufacturing company producing it. No matter how clever we get, entropy always takes its toll, in every situation and in every location. A better chance of success awaited the man who seriously proposed that the total farming capacity of the United Kingdom should be turned over to marigold production and that the aircraft gas turbines manufactured by the organisation I then worked with should have hoppers added to feed the marigold seeds into the engine's combustion chambers for burning!

From his microscopic observations, Clausius used the universe as his model when he drew the conclusions 'the energy of the Universe is constant: the entropy of the Universe tends towards a maximum'. Clausius had put into specific terms what scientists had been groping towards for over half a century.

It is this pronouncement, 'the entropy of the Universe tends to a maximum', that is of vital importance. In making it, Clausius did not refer to individual processes taking place in the universe, neither did he consider different theories of its creation, evolution and direction. He didn't need to. All that was necessary for his statement to hold true was that all processes should be irreversible. In fact, beyond the page of theory that the reluctant student of thermodynamics has thrust upon him, there are no processes which are reversible, which means that none is perfect. It is evident in our lives, our bodies, our gardens and our homes: things decay. So, both within our everyday experience and beyond into the most esoteric fields of scientific endeavour, the irreversible process decrees an increase of entropy, thus substantiating Clausius' declaration.

Crucial as this is in the working of the cosmos, Clausius' description of the Second Law is also pivotal in the development of our search for the *how* and the *why* of the universe and for eternity itself.

Having broken free from the idea that fire was an element, the thoughts of scientists had advanced from the specific and localised — a steam engine occupying a very small volume in the whole of space — to the general and universal. It had been discovered that there were two laws of thermodynamics. Our history shows that they demanded obedience, not only in a heat engine as an engineer would recognise it, but everywhere in the universe. From the action of amino acids observed under a microscope to the influences on stars in the furthest known galaxies of the universe viewed through a telescope, these laws reigned supreme. Before them, all nature had to bow.

CHAPTER FIVE

SLINGING THE ARROWS

I T'S A LONG WAY from a nineteenth-century steam engine for threshing hay to a twentieth-century ion rocket for propelling a space probe, or from an abacus to a main-frame computer. Ingenuity in devising new equipment to meet civilisation's needs is without limit — and the equipment becomes more complex as it is more refined. But it is a curious thing that, however ingenious the design or efficient its operation, every mechanism that man has built brings, with its operation, an inevitable increase in entropy.

With Carnot, we saw that the steam engine's operation lost energy — but we might have reckoned that to be a result of a general inefficiency, resulting from a lack of knowledge of modern techniques in design, manufacture or operation such as we have today. Such slackness in manufacture that 'only a worn shilling' could be fitted between the cylinder and its piston would be bound to be costly in efficiency. The limitations of nineteenth-century engineering did make their contribution, but only to add to the fundamental increase in entropy that nature declares must accompany any process.

And this increase in entropy is not reserved just for big objects. Chemical actions seen through a microscope are constrained in an identical manner — heat is dumped irretrievably — and this means that entropy is increased. The creation of protein from amino acids or the formation of complex polymers like deoxyribonucleic acid — DNA — the molecule which carries the hereditary information from one generation to another in a family and does much to form our characters, all involve an entropy increase. Our domestic appliances, refrigerator, vacuum cleaner and coffee-grinder, as well as our bodies, generate entropy which adds to the irreversible trend in the whole cosmic order. On every occasion that energy is used in whatever form, it runs to a lower level of usefulness and hence a higher level of disorder. It is rather like a stream tumbling down a hill-side in a series of cascading falls, becoming progressively less valuable as an energy source, but with an increasing disorder or turbulence; that is higher entropy.

This is the global statement to cover the whole of a so-called system to which the Second Law of thermodynamics is applied. But the Second Law makes no particular demand upon any individual sector within the system. In fact, it is possible to have a local reduction of entropy in one region at the expense of more entropy elsewhere in the system, rather like moving furniture from one room in a house to another. The Second Law is satisfied so long as there is, overall, an entropy increase — an additional piece of furniture for the house. Bearing in mind that low entropy indicates an orderliness and the availability of useful energy, we can see many examples of low entropy maintenance about us. But there is always a cost in thermodynamic terms: energy must be fed into the system.

A clear example of this is our earth, which depends upon the sun for its life. A continual flow of energy from the sun maintains the overall orderliness in the earth's processes. If the sun was switched off — we have already observed that we would know about it approximately eight minutes after the event — things could not continue as normal. From the moment that the news reached us to say that the sun had gone out, processes on the earth would begin to run down. The radiation of heat from the earth into space would continue for a while, dumping heat to the universe until there was no more to dump. Chaos would be the eventual result as the temperature of everything descended to a uniform level which is the background temperature of the universe — very, very cold. Entropy would have reached a maximum on the earth and life would have long since ceased.

Maintained low entropy is seen in our homes with the refrigerator. Switching it on reduces its entropy as the temperature is lowered. But energy, electricity in this case, must be fed in. When it has reached its cold operation point, the refrigerator is maintained in a low temperature/low entropy condition by continuing to feed energy in.

The picture we have is similar to a passenger on the 'down' side of an escalator. If, in passing an advertisement on the escalator side-wall, he became engrossed in it, he could stop his descent by walking back up the escalator at the same rate the escalator is descending. To maintain his position, he is using energy. That is the parallel to the earth absorbing heat from the sun to maintain its general level of order. If he then wanted to read another advertisement further up the escalator path, he could walk up even more quickly to reach it: evidently he would have to go up faster than the escalator was taking him down. That is the parallel to switching on the refrigerator to get it to its operational temperature.

But, always, energy is fed in and lost. The passenger gets hot while treading the stairs and the heat goes to the atmosphere as he sweats. The entropy of the surroundings is increasing in consequence. This is like the radiation of heat from the earth's surface, or the heat being dumped from the refrigerator through its radiator.

The current concern over the environment with the realisation of the 'greenhouse effect' is an interesting example of entropy increase. At the time of writing this manuscript (1989), meteorologists report that the six hottest summers in history worldwide have been in the last decade. In consequence, there is the threat of a general warming of the earth that will upset the ecological balance of nature. Already it is reported that ocean levels are rising due to melting polar ice-caps. Areas that historically have been temperate are becoming arid whereas, because the climate is reacting unfavourably, others are suffering storms of unheard of severity. What is happening?

In order to maintain conditions on the earth's surface at a generally constant level, the total heat received from the sun added to that released in industrial processes on the earth must be exactly balanced by the heat radiated to space from the earth. This is the normal activity of a hot body in cold surroundings, and against the cold background of space the earth behaves as a hot body.

The rules describing the radiation of heat tell us that the greater the temperature difference, in our case the hotter the earth, the more heat is radiated. Conversely, the less the temperature difference, that is the cooler the earth, the less heat is lost in radiation.

The system is therefore to some extent self-compensating. Historically, this mechanism has usefully maintained the balance for the earth and its temperature range has remained largely unchanged.

But the laws of heat transfer also have something to say about the medium through which the heat is being transferred. On a cold night in bed, we pull the covers closer or maybe add another blanket or comforter. We know that this will keep us warmer. In other words, the heat loss is reduced by introducing a barrier to heat transfer and the bedclothes are that barrier. In this way, we demonstrate our innate understanding of heat transfer and we know that with more bedclothes on we maintain the necessary temperature difference for comfort between our bodies, producing heat, and the air outside of the bed.

The atmosphere around the earth serves as the blanket and its heat transparency allows the heat at the earth's surface, both that absorbed from the sun and that converted into heat by other processes on the earth, to be emitted to space. The atmosphere has, however, recently been changing and, because of industrial exhaust of one sort or another — and particularly the burning of the immense rain forests — it is absorbing such gases as carbon dioxide and nitrous oxide. Their effect on the atmosphere is to reduce the radiated rate of heat transfer into space: they are, in effect, the additional blanket used on the cold night in bed.

Curiously, the presence of these gases in the atmosphere does not reduce the radiated heat absorbed from the sun, so they behave as a one-way valve, letting heat in but resisting it getting out. To reach an equilibrium situation with these gases present — that is, one in which the seasons again become cyclic and there is no variation in temperature range from year to year — involves a higher temperature difference, that is, a higher earth temperature. If then the atmosphere remained in this new state with the new constituents of carbon dioxide and so on, the result would be a generally higher temperature at the surface of the earth, but conditions would be repeatable as they were before the problem began.

The concern of the moment is that things may not settle down in this way. Further industrialisation and deforestation (the forests are nature's way of absorbing carbon dioxide) and attempts to counter the effects of higher temperature — air-conditioning is an example — will make for more 'greenhouse gases' in the atmosphere, so there could be a run-away situation.

The problem to the environmentalist is the changing atmosphere. To us though, this is a clear example of increased entropy in a system: the higher temperatures experienced represent energy which is disordered and cannot be usefully employed. It is entropy that can no longer escape to the universe outside.

It is said that in a few years the weather conditions in the United Kingdom will be those we currently recognise as Mediterranean as the earth continues to heat up. Venus, which has very high surface temperatures and an entirely hostile atmosphere, has now become of greater interest since it has been suggested that the earth's future is Venus' present. This process has sometimes been called the heat death, though the term usually refers to the condition of low, not high, temperature at the earth's surface due to entropy in the cosmos reaching a maximum.

Interestingly, both the low temperature scenario presented earlier in this chapter — a condition when no energy remains in a useful form — and the high temperature 'greenhouse effect' climate towards which we appear to be heading, represent high entropy situations. We conclude, therefore, that entropy is not related to a particular temperature band but only to the useful availability of the energy within the system.

Whatever happens, the approach of a heat death through low temperature conditions or a suffocation with a high temperature atmosphere, cosmic entropy is increasing inexorably. That is what prompted Sir Arthur Eddington, sometime Professor of Astronomy at the University of Cambridge, to say:

> The law that entropy always increases — the Second Law of thermodynamics — holds, I think, the supreme position among the laws of nature. If someone points out to you that your pet theory of the universe is in disagreement with Maxwell's equations — then so much the worse for Maxwell's equations. If it is found to be contradicted by observation — well, these experimentalists do bungle things sometimes. But if your theory is found to be against the Second Law of thermodynamics I can give you no hope: there is nothing for it but to collapse in deepest humiliation.

*   *   *

Because of the Second Law we see that the cost of maintaining the earth at a *higher* temperature than space is paid for in increased entropy. But there is also a cost in keeping a refrigerator at a *lower* temperature than its surroundings — increased entropy. This is the dissymmetry of nature of which we spoke in chapter 4. Entropy goes, overall, in one direction only. The Second Law has this unique feature that whatever the process, in whatever direction, entropy always goes its own way. Other laws of nature are different. Light reflects from a surface at the angle it approaches it: the formation of water from oxygen and hydrogen and the hydrolysis, or decomposition, of water into its constituents of oxygen and hydrogen are governed by the same chemical equations.

Since the Second Law has this unchanging arrow of direction, it is sometimes said to define the direction of time. Time and entropy advance together and the consequences of this are very important. Every process on which our lives depend results in an entropy increase, so we can only proceed in one direction — time advances and we get older. The time machine taking us back to another age, fanciful as it may be to science fiction buffs, is an impossibility. The only time machine that we may know is the one that guarantees our aging process: the arrow of time is fixed.

During the 1960s, a lecture by the astronomer Fred Hoyle at the Royal Society suggested the possibility of sending a radio message back through time. There is no difficulty in sending radio messages forward in time — that is what normally happens. A signal may be sent to a distant point where there is a reflector which returns it immediately to a receiver set alongside the transmitter. It arrives some time after it has been sent out, the time dictated by the distance and the speed of light. The message has gone forward in time. The same electromagnetic laws that had made this possible, it was argued, could then be harnessed to project a signal back into history.

The picture we have is, of course, bizarre. If only he had a tuned receiver, King Harold could have been warned of the results of William the Conqueror's invasion and history might have been rewritten. In fact, we could reorganise history until it matched exactly what appealed to us. The proposal was not only bizarre, it was impossible because, apart from any other restrictions there might be, sending a radio signal involves the use of energy upon which there is an inevitable tax — entropy — whose arrow points in one direction only. Entropy and time advance together.

*   *   *

Aging has many disadvantages to us, but it also has some advantages of which experience is one. Experience builds up memory, data acquired over a period of time and stored for recall as necessary. Our value to society is largely due to what we have learned by experience, apprenticeships, academic training and quite simply, passing through the school of life. Now, it is quite obvious that memory works in one direction only — we know what has happened but we can't remember what will happen. What is the connection between memory, entropy and time?

Memory is increased with information given. The gossip who is able to tell us the darkest secrets of our next-door neighbour is passing information, data, on to us that we can store in our memories — and probably will if it is really damning! The more information we have, the more our memories grow. A person isolated in a darkened cave may have plenty of time to reflect, using memory to great advantage, but his store of memory is not going to grow appreciably — little by way of information is coming his way.

Now, entropy has been connected to memory in the following manner. The greater the entropy of a system, the greater the randomness in it. As an example let us consider two different substances in a container, a red liquid and a blue liquid, kept apart by a thin membrane. The organised structure seen in their separation is regarded as a condition of low entropy. If the membrane is broken so that the liquids can mix, they will do so and eventually the container will be filled with a uniform purple liquid. All the particles of red have mixed with the blue and those of blue have mixed with the red. That thoroughly mixed state, when no more can occur, is a condition of high entropy.

But every particle carries a piece of information to declare that it is red or, alternatively, blue. Now, if an individual capable of interpreting the data was standing in the container, he would, in encountering the particles that came his way, receive information to build up his memory. With increasing entropy, he meets more particles and thus more data: his memory is further enhanced.

Memory and entropy are increasing in the same direction. In different situations particles may, of course, carry other information, histories that announce that they were mined from a diamond mine — they are diamonds — or that, as specks of rust, they were part of the Titanic.

If we alter the picture somewhat, replacing particles with people, each carrying some item of news to feed our memories, the application of this picture becomes clearer. In a crowded airport terminal like Chicago or Heathrow, the milling crowds would have a lot to tell us if we were inclined to listen.

Yet this argument is incomplete. We cannot conclude that constant entropy conditions, or a reduction of entropy, yield no information. Indeed, in such situations, the observer still meets particles carrying information. Additions are still being made to his memory.

A column of soldiers marching in step is a low-entropy parallel to our crowded airport, but we would have plenty to learn from them as they marched by.

Further, if the arrow of memory has its direction dictated by the arrow of entropy in a system, not only would a constant entropy situation result in no memory, but a reducing entropy situation would inevitably mean that we could only remember what will happen tomorrow while having a total blank regarding yesterday's events. At first sight, tomorrow's news looks very attractive for the man who backs horses or dabbles on the Stock Exchange, but the winnings would have little value since the lucky investor would not have memory or experience to help him decide what to do with it, neither would he later be able to recall the benefit gained from his wealth!

Ah, but we can't test this hypothesis because entropy always increases, we say. We can, in specific situations. Recall that we can maintain entropy constant or even reduce it locally within a system: the refrigerator was an example. Let's put our potential millionaire into the refrigerator and see what happens. As the temperature is reduced to the operating level, does he forget everything about his past and suddenly recall that an unannounced war coming in the Middle East next week will devalue his investments so that he is motivated to sell? When the operating temperature is reached and the entropy is constant in his environment, does he have no memory at all, either of the past or the future? Of course not. When we drag him from his uncomfortable position we can expect that his over-riding comment would relate to how cold he had been in there. His arrow of memory is, in fact, in the same direction as before — he recalls the past. If that was not so, the life of a man working in the cold-store of a wholesale butcher would be very unusual!

But entropy has, overall, increased to maintain the cold environment of the refrigerator, so perhaps he was not really in an entropy-reducing environment. Remember that memory was related to meeting information — the red or the blue particles in the original container. Their movement was the total experience of the man in the container: like the person existing in the darkened cave, he had no idea of what was happening outside, so the change of entropy out there, whether increasing rapidly or slowly, whether stationary or reducing, meant nothing to him. It was his immediate environment that controlled him.

The arrow of memory is therefore not determined by the arrow of entropy. In a normal situation the two are connected only by the arrow of time. Memory grows as time advances, but also, because of the demands of the Second Law, entropy too grows with time. Time is the arrow that fixes the direction of development of entropy and memory separately.

Man is constrained to live in an entropy-increasing environment solely because his life is experienced in the domain of advancing time and it happens that this is the direction in which entropy moves towards its maximum. In the matter of the movement of entropy then, man becomes a detached observer. If there is a case for decreasing entropy, he can make a judgement in the normal way. If entropy can only increase he can draw his conclusions. These are what we now examine.

*   *   *

As time advances, memory increases. It's the way we work. Further, entropy increase has a unique direction: it grows with time. That's the way the world works.

Must this be so? Is it important anyway? Could we not be taking different areas of science — thermodynamics, psychology, astronomy — and lacing them together to make an abstract point which doesn't really apply to life? Or do these arrows have real meaning that addresses, in some way, how the cosmos works and why we are here? What would be the situation if the arrows didn't follow this protocol? What would happen if the entropy arrow was reversed so that time advance saw a reduction of entropy?

Man needs energy. This comes from the food he eats and is used for work, pleasure — all the activities of life. Some, about 150 watts (the unit of electrical power — in this case the power is equivalent to a couple of normal electric light bulbs), is lost to the atmosphere because his body temperature is above that of the surroundings. This heat loss has uses, for we can warm one another up by being close together. Members of the Department of Architecture of a famous university, in demonstrating how good they were in their discipline, determined to design their own departmental building. The architecture was *avant-garde* but so was the heating. The main lecture theatre could seat about a hundred students which the architects determined gave them 15 kilowatts of heat, adequate to keep its temperature at the right level. So the theatre was built with no heating. Alas, the academic architects forgot one thing. The first lecture of the day began in the cold, yesterday's heat having been dissipated in accordance with the Second Law, so while generously adding their personal contributions of heat to warm up the department, the students were in danger of expiring through frostbite!

This heat loss is because man is hot-blooded. He must be, for otherwise he would be with snakes and reptiles towards the bottom, not at the top, of the scale of nature's beings. So, in order to allow his physiology and intelligence to operate appropriately, he maintains a relatively warm body. Some of the energy he absorbs in food must, because of the temperature difference, be dissipated to the atmosphere. Man, of necessity, is an entropy increaser.

Even so, must he live in an entropy-increasing environment?

An entropy-increasing world is one that sees things cool down in a predictable manner. This world has characteristics including friction, which is an energy dissipater, decay and increasing disorder — all signs of entropy increase. But let's imagine a world of entropy reduction. Our entropy-decreasing world would reverse things. Rather than cool down because of heat dissipation, things would warm up because heat would gather spontaneously. But what things? We don't know. Maybe the seat you are sitting on would get hot quite suddenly or the kettle would boil when you didn't particularly want it to. Because experience is used in circumstances which are to some extent predictable, your experience and hence your memory would be of no value in this world.

It would be a world without friction, and while that sounds admirable, there wouldn't be brakes for vehicles, neither could we stand safely on any surface without fear of slipping over.

There would be no need of a manufacturing industry: products would happen spontaneously as order appeared from disorder. That seems good but we don't know what products would happen, neither would we be able to control their production. A world with adequate washing-machines is one thing, but the inability to stop washing machines being made when everybody has several could create storage problems! The unfortunate ability of the Sorcerer's Apprentice to create an endless supply of porridge was a violation of the laws of thermodynamics!

Clearly, a world of decreasing entropy comprises a run-away system with no control. It is not our world and hence, it is not our universe. For life to be recognisable, entropy must increase with time and that is the reason for us having useful memories. Life as we know it is an entropy increaser and we can only live in an entropy-increasing environment.

It is this fundamental feature of existence, entropy increasing with time, which we shall apply in the next chapter as we look at some cosmological models. And it is the application of this 'supreme law', as Sir Arthur Eddington called it, that will divide the likely from the unlikely, drawing us back towards our prime question *why*? Which of the cosmological models is likely? The Second Law will guide us. What way is the cosmos going, if any way at all? Let the Second Law point the way.

CHAPTER SIX

PULSES, BANGS AND OTHER THINGS

THE STORY IS TOLD (by me, because I was there) of the archaeologist who had recently been involved in a 'dig' at a neolithic site close to where I live. He was exhibiting a number of pieces which had been labelled as axe-heads, knife blades and so on, but aroused suspicion in me since they appeared identical with a garden full of the stuff I had discovered when digging my way through my own undergrowth. I asked him the age of his finds and was told that they were 9 million years old. Upon putting the further question, evidently interpreted as impertinent, how did he know that, his answer was, 'Because I say so.'

The voice of authority does not invite question, certainly not challenge, but when different authorities give different accounts of one event, enquiry is inevitable. Certainly, there appear to be several mutually exclusive cosmological theories, each giving a somewhat different account of the probable beginnings, current state and eventual destiny of the universe. Irrespective of these differences, any speculation in a scientific context about where we are going as a universe, or where we have been in the past, must be based upon what we can establish of the universe — its shape, characteristics and measurable timescale — as it is now. But we also need to keep in mind the warning at the beginning of Stephen Hawking's book, *A Brief History of Time*: 'A theory is just a model of the Universe, or a restricted part of it — It exists only in our minds and does not have any other reality.' In case we conclude that this makes scientific endeavour redundant, Hawking justifies the usefulness of a theory: 'It must accurately describe a large class of observations — and it must make definite predictions about the results of any future observations.' What accurate description of the cosmos can we give to which may be added a range of predictive, or retrospective, theories?

*   *   *

Edwin Hubble was a lawyer. A student of Roman and English law at the University of Oxford, he practised as a lawyer for a year before — like 70% of all law graduates — he decided to do something else. The 'something else' was a career in experimental astronomy and a particular interest in galaxies — vast collections of stars set in the sky like huge well-lighted cities of which the Milky Way is our own 'city'. In 1929 his observations of galaxies were formulated into a law that was revelatory to man about the universe in which he lives.

The distances of galaxies cannot be determined by any of the usual means but are estimated by measuring their brightness; the less bright, the further away they are. Light, such as that from stars, can be broken down into frequencies: low-frequency light is red, so a British mail box reflects low-frequency light, while the colour blue, such as the light on a police car, is of high frequency. White light comprises all the frequencies from low to high — that is why it is made up of all the rainbow colours, as Leonardo and Newton discovered. When Hubble measured the light emitting from various galaxies he discovered that the frequency was always and unexpectedly shifted towards the red end of the spectrum. Further, the shift for different galaxies wasn't always the same, yet there was a pattern in his observations: the further the galaxy away from him, the redder the light that he measured.

Red or blue shift in light frequencies is similar to an acoustic effect we can all check. If we stand on a railway platform, the sound of an approaching train can be clearly heard. As it passes us, while the noise level remains high, the tone drops sharply [Fig 6.1]. This is particularly noticeable if the train is sounding its whistle or, in another example, if we listen to the siren of an ambulance passing us. What we are hearing is a contraction of wavelength, that is an increase of frequency, as the vehicle approaches, and a stretching of wavelength, that is a reduction of frequency and thus a lowering of tone as it recedes from us, an effect entirely due to the movement of the train or ambulance relative to us. It is called the Doppler effect, after the Austrian physicist who first predicted it.

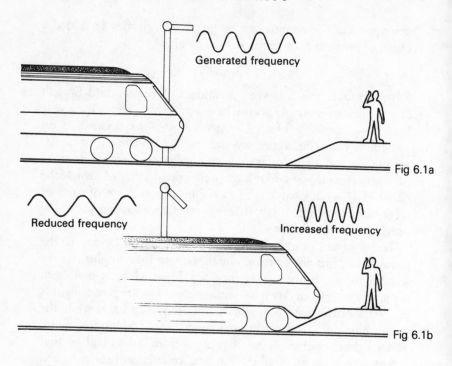

Generated frequency

Fig 6.1a

Reduced frequency

Increased frequency

Fig 6.1b

Red shifted light

Blue shifted light

Fig 6.1c

Fig 6.1 The Doppler Effect

In fig 6.1a, the train stands stationary outside the station and the listener hears the noise from the train at the generated frequency. The effect of the train's movement is to compress the forward-radiating sound waves (increasing their frequency) and stretch the rearward-generated sound waves (reducing their frequency). The listener hears a sound at a higher pitch as the train approaches and as it passes, the pitch drops.

Light behaves similarly. In fig 6.1c, those waves radiating ahead of an object — say a galaxy — are seen at a higher frequency (blue shift) while those behind a receding object are at a lower frequency (red shift).

There is a similar effect with light waves. If the object emitting the light is travelling towards us the light appears bluer, if it is receding from us, the light appears redder.

Hubble noted that the light emitted from galaxies had a

characteristic red shift indicating that they were receding from him. The greater the distance to the galaxy, the greater the recession speed. The uniformity of his data put paid to the earlier thought that the galaxies may have been moving about the heavens in a random sort of way. But his measurements were open to two interpretations: either the earth was at the centre of a universe that was fleeing from it, or the whole of the universe was expanding so that the space between all the galaxies was growing. The former idea was dispensed with: why should more distant galaxies be travelling faster in that picture? So there emerged an interpretation, which is now accepted, that the universe is expanding, the space between galaxies growing in such a way that the distant galaxies move away from us more quickly than neighbouring ones.

The picture is quite simple. In a two-dimensional parallel we see this effect by dropping a pebble into a still pond. A circular wave system radiates from the point where the pebble hits the water. Three ripples travelling with the wave are initially close, because the wave is small in circumference. As the wave radiates, the ripples move with it, receding from each other, the distance between neighbours growing less quickly than that between neighbours-but-one [Fig 6.2].

That is a two-dimensional picture representing a three-dimensional effect. In three dimensions, we replace the pebble in the surface of the water by a spherical balloon being inflated. Points drawn on the surface of the balloon can represent galaxies which move apart as the balloon gets larger, the distance between them growing in the same manner as the ripples on the water wave. The neighbouring-but-one point thus recedes from any nominated point at a higher rate than the neighbouring point [Fig 6.3]. With a perversity that is sometimes present — and seems to have been planted to defeat our own cleverness — there is an exception to the red shift picture indicating a uniformly expanding universe. Andromeda, the galaxy closest to ours, has a blue shift. It is not receding. It is approaching us. Since it is about 2.5 million light-years from us, a collision is not however imminent!

Hubble was able to get data from galaxies whose distance from the earth was approaching a thousand million (a billion) light years and he found that the growth in speed measured using the red shift increased uniformly with distance, every increment of increased

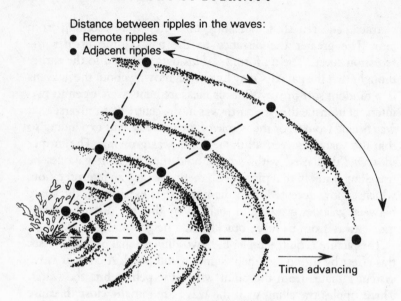

Fig 6.2 The Pebble in the Pond

A pebble falling into a pond causes a series of radiating waves. If ripples were carried by the waves they would move apart from each other, as this figure indicates, but those that are remote from each other would separate more quickly than those that are adjacent. If the pebble splash represents a big bang and the ripples are galaxies, the resultant expansion would create greater red shift between the outermost galaxies than adjacent ones.

Fig 6.3 The Expanding Space

The effects seen in two dimensions in fig 6.2 can be repeated in three dimensions. Fig 6.3 shows an inflating balloon, dots on the surface separating as it grows. Dots which are remote from each other separate more quickly than those that are close, giving the picture of a red-shifted universe if the dots are taken to be galaxies.

distance being matched by an increment of frequency shift. This became known as the Hubble Law. Since then, advances in the astronomers' tool-kit have made possible measurements of galaxies up to nearly six billion light years away — and the Hubble Law still holds true. Not only were things in the universe changing, as Tycho Brahe had discovered in seeing his supernova, but so was the universe itself.

But why, if Newton's theory of universal gravitation holds true, does the universe expand? Gravity is attractive and should be drawing all the bodies in the universe together. Since it is expanding now, will there be a time when gravity will exert its authority: expansion will turn into contraction? These are the questions that have prompted speculation of the universe's origins and fate which we now examine.

*   *   *

Rather like the pebble in the pond, could there have been an incident to begin the expansion of the universe? Or were there other forces at work to create this expansive movement?

A challenging idea to suggest other forces appeared in the late 1940s. Three scientists, Fred Hoyle, Herman Bondi and Thomas Gold, it is said, had one evening in 1946 been watching a film together. The plot, which was a ghost story, led to a conclusion that was identical to the starting point. This had the obvious inference that the film should be exactly repeated, a loop from which the observer could never escape. (Today's blockbuster films, when successful, are followed by Mark II and Mark III versions and so on, where the plot is, in any case, virtually identical!) In a discussion following the film, the proposition was put that this could be a model of the cosmos — a continual cycle which, to the observer, had no beginning or end.

The essence of the resulting picture was of matter at the outer edge of the universe disappearing and, towards the centre, galactic clouds forming which condensed into new galaxies. As with the arrival of a further passenger in a crowded train or street-car, the other occupants making room for him and adjusting their positions to suit, so the rest of the universe expanded to make room for the newly arrived galaxy. The result was the steady state, or continuous creation model of the universe, but one which had the necessary expansion indicated by Hubble's work.

Controversy was generated around this proposal which stood in stark contrast to the hitherto accepted ideas that included a moment of creation. Hoyle's first paper on the subject was rejected, but subsequently the proposition enjoyed a season of popularity. It comprised an attempt to dispense with the idea of a creation moment. Stanley Jaki dismissed the theory as the most daring trick ever given a scientific veneer. Having recently attended a lecture on Cosmology by Professor Jaki — given in Italian which I understand very imperfectly — and noted his expressive manner, I can believe that Professor Jaki's comment was made with some conviction!

Can this be a credible picture? There is some evidence of galaxies undergoing a forming process. But a model of continuous creation, in which events exactly repeat like the ghost story, violates the Second Law of thermodynamics. Even if matter did disintegrate at the outer edge of the universe to reform, more or less where it had been during an earlier part of the epoch, it could not do so in an identical manner, entropy having taken its toll. There would be a continual drift in the universe towards a state of higher entropy and if that happened, random energy would put up the temperature level of the universe progressively making less energy available to drive the mechanism of continuous creation. This would continue until no energy at all remained for the purpose of driving the system. Continuous creation cannot work. There are other reasons why the theory has been discounted, but even if they played no part, the increasing entropy principle would be enough to ensure that the system wound down.

A further proposal relates to the expansion of the universe. Will the moment come when it stops expanding and the galaxies, under the control of a mutual gravitational attraction, begin to coalesce — the explosion becomes an implosion? That depends upon the mass of material in the universe and hence the strength of the gravitational attraction as well as the current rate of expansion in the universe. It is possible to assess the amount of luminescent material in the Universe — we can see that through telescopes, planets in our solar system, stars and galaxies beyond being visible. In addition there are many radio sources which cannot be seen with the eye, but radio telescopes, doing the same sort of job as optical telescopes in a different frequency range, can be used to make an assessment of the mass involved. Beyond that, there is a mass of 'dark' matter, material that has no signature in the range of our instruments but which, because it exists, must make a contribution to the total gravitational force field in the cosmos. Only if we know how much dark matter there is, will it be possible to say how much matter exists in the universe, the resultant gravitational forces involved and whether implosion will therefore occur.

Let us suppose it does. An expanding universe, beginning from an immensely dense concentration of matter which is hurled outwards at the beginning, returns to become an immensely dense concentration of matter. As the reverse of the Big Bang this is sometimes called the Big Crunch.

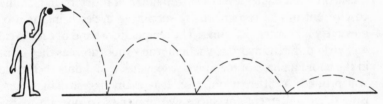

Fig 6.4a A bouncing ball with the effect of entropy

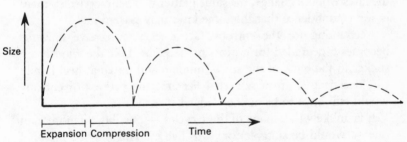

Fig 6.4b A cyclic universe with the effect of entropy

Fig 6.4 The Bouncing Ball

Potential and kinetic energy are repeatedly exchanged as the ball bounces after being thrown by the player in fig 6.4a. Entropy takes its toll and available energy progressively reduces until the ball no longer bounces. The picture of a universe following a series of cycles of expansion and contraction gives a similar pattern. Entropy takes its toll again and the process runs down, each cycle being at a higher temperature with the increase of entropy, just as a squash-racquets ball gets hot in play (even hotter than the players!). As with the ball's trajectory in fig 6.4a, the process in the universe is constrained to have an end and a beginning.

Having reassembled at a point as a supremely dense mass, in the same pattern as it began, there appears to be no reason why the cycle should not be repeated. Once again, an expanding universe results, only to suffer the same fate as before. The cycle continues for ever, rather like a bouncing rubber ball that never loses its bounce. We can call this the oscillating, or pulsing, theory. But even the best rubber balls stop bouncing eventually, because entropy is interested in the behaviour of rubber balls. So too with the pulsing system of successive universes — entropy takes its toll [Fig 6.4]. Cycles of expansion and contraction cannot take place in an identical manner, simply because of the dissymmetry of the entropy law — entropy increases in the expansion phase: it also increases during the contraction phase, so that the cycle, when finished, is at a higher level of entropy than at the start. In fact, the cost of entropy is recognised by successive cycles being at progressively higher temperatures. The temperature band of each cycle will yield different hydrogen/helium/iron proportions as they distil in the cooling phase of the universe expansion and thus each cycle will produce a different universe. It is even suggested that there isn't the requirement for successive universes to operate to the same set of laws. Nevertheless, even if there is no guarantee that the laws will not change, the same matter will be re-cycled so there is some confidence that the same laws may govern it.

Accounting for the entropy factor, each successive universe becomes a degraded form of its predecessor. Like the windscreen sticker in the back of the small, humble and down-at-heel family car, declaring 'I am a re-cycled Ferrari', the process of entropy would still have to be acknowledged.

It is unlikely that many of these cycles — possibly no more than one — would be suitable for us to live in. This may be the one! More important though, if successive cycles are not identical but follow a trend — progressively higher temperature bands as the Second Law dictates — then it follows that we cannot have an infinite series of cycles. There are only two ways in which such a process could be infinite: either every cycle is identical with its forebear — that would call for cycles in which there is no entropy increase, an impossibility — or cycles in which the temperature band increases, followed by cycles in which the temperature band decreases, maintaining overall the same temperature range. That would call for some cycles in which the entropy decreases — an impossibility. We are left with one conclusion. A series of expansion/contraction cycles of the universe must have started at some time. There must have been a beginning.

For those who are concerned that they may find it a little crowded as the universe contracts, if it does, they can be assured that it won't begin doing so for many millions of years. But better news is to hand. It appears, so far as can be deduced from current calculations, that the rate of expansion of the universe is just high enough to overcome the arresting effect of gravity — the universe may, then, continue to expand. In his book *Superforce*, British physicist, Paul Davies, relates 'the way in which the strength of the explosion was exactly matched to the gravitational power of the Cosmos such that the expansion rate today lies very close to the borderline between re-collapse and rapid dispersal'. He continues by claiming that inflation can give no other expansion rate than the one that is observed. If this is the case, there can be no pulsing or even a single re-collapse in the universe.

*　　*　　*

It was Aristotle who first proposed a universe without beginning or end — an eternal continuum in which the cosmos was an unchanging entity. We have seen that astronomers from Brahe onwards progressively dismantled Aristotle's astronomy. But maintaining Aristotle's idea of an eternal universe, a succession of cosmic models contain the ingredient of a universe without beginning or end. The most recent is that of Stephen Hawking whose ingenious mathematical model suggests that the universe might 'really [be] self-contained, having no boundary or edge, it would have neither beginning nor end: it would simply be.' He adds the rhetorical question, 'What place, then, for a creator?'

Hawking's model relies upon a mathematical technique involving the use of imaginary or complex numbers. Imaginary numbers have been known about since the sixteenth century, but they were at first thought to be nothing other than a curiosity without any application. It was Geronimo Cardano, Cardan as he is generally known, who in the early sixteenth century found that the solutions of certain equations involved taking the square root of negative numbers. He knew this was an impossibility. Yet his solutions

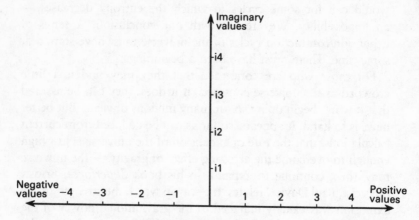

Fig 6.5 Imaginary Numbers
If the meeting point of the lines in the above graph is taken to have zero value, then
those to the right are positive and to the left, negative. Vertical values are neither
positive nor negative: they are imaginary. This figure is usually referred to as an
Argand diagram after the mathematician JR Argand, who first published an
account of this graphical representation in 1806.

evaded him without recourse to these numbers which he regarded
as 'sophistic', 'as subtle as they are useless'. Useless they were not,
but it took a long time to understand their value.

The easiest way to picture an imaginary number is to consider a
sheet of paper upon which is drawn a line to the right of an
originating point and another to its left. If we take distances along
the line to the right to represent positive numbers, then that to the
left can represent negative numbers. In this picture or graph,
movement at right angles to the line, say vertically upwards,
represents the values of imaginary numbers [Fig 6.5].

If they are imaginary what on earth is their use? Asking that
question puts us in good company, that of men like Simon Stevin,
a sixteenth-century engineer, and Gottfried Leibniz, a seventeenth-
century mathematician. With his practical engineering turn of
mind — he popularised decimal algebra, using a notation all of his
own, and introduced double-entry book-keeping to the Low
Countries — Stevin said of imaginary numbers, 'There are enough
legitimate things to work on without need to get busy on uncertain
matter.' Leibniz, who was narrowly beaten by Newton in his claim
to have invented the calculus, held the view that imaginary

numbers were 'a sort of amphibian, half way between existence and non-existence'. Looking to his experience as a Christian, he drew the rather strange parallel that these numbers resembled 'in this respect, the Holy Ghost in Christian Theology'. He possibly had in mind that, like the Holy Ghost who can't be seen but nevertheless has his effect, so it is with imaginary numbers.

Surprising as it would have been to Stevin, it was in a branch of engineering that imaginary numbers were to find great use; wherever wave phenomena were under investigation. These 'sophistic' numbers are used to investigate the patterns of waves which are out of phase with one another (that is, their peaks and troughs do not occur at the same time) and the frequency of the peaks may be different for different waves. Oscillations in cables such as overhead electrical wires excited by the wind are an example. The cables of national electrical grid systems, strung between pylons at considerable distance from each other, sometimes have movements which are very complex, waves of different type being superimposed on each other to make a strange pattern of movement. A winter evening in one of England's windy quarters, East Anglia, is memorable to me for the sight of brilliant green flashes lighting up the night sky as, around the horizon, power lines shorted out against each other, touching in an apparently random manner to produce prodigious sparks with no fixed pattern of frequency. But there was a pattern hidden among the many wave frequencies the cables were experiencing, and to evaluate them a mathematical device was needed that could manage the analysis. Many people will recall the famous film of the disintegration of the Tacoma Narrows Bridge in the 1940s when, excited by cross-winds, the suspension bridge began to oscillate in a complex series of movements culminating in its destruction. Pictures taken looking along the road on the bridge showed vertical and lateral waves of varying frequency running along from one end of the bridge to the other.

Analysis of such patterns, wherever vibrations or waves occur, is made possible by using imaginary numbers. And it is in this manner that they are used by Stephen Hawking. The reason lies in Hawking's observation that in an initial phase of the universe, 'the gravitational field becomes so strong that quantum gravitational effects become important — a quantum theory of gravity is thus necessary to discuss the very early stages of the universe.'

Imaginary numbers, because of their name and the fact that they aren't like ordinary numbers, are difficult to envisage: eight apples or three cats, because the numbers can be connected with something real, do not give us a problem. So the imaginary number has acquired a mystique all of its own. If we regard it simply as a device to enable a mathematical calculation to be done, a means to an end, it loses its special aura. After all, few people understand how a pocket calculator works, but it no longer commands a particular respect because it is so commonly used: it is a device to help in doing some arithmetic; a means to an end.

We can recall from Chapter 3 that the result of Planck's quantum theory and the uncertainty principle that went with it, meant that we could not be certain of the details of particle trajectories and velocities. A particle searches out every possible trajectory: exactly how it moves is not known. Calculations become a matter of probability and the probability of a particle being at any point is related to the way that the sum of the trajectories is added up. This in turn depends upon the magnitude and the phase of the waves that define the various trajectories. In adding them up, the same principle used by the vibrations engineer is employed. Thus, calculations in the quantum gravity field described by Professor Hawking involve imaginary numbers. The dimension whose imaginary component he uses is Time — hence imaginary time features in his work. Its use, he describes as 'a mathematical device (or trick) to calculate answers about real spacetime'. It is the means to the end.

In Hawking's resulting model it emerges that spacetime can be finite but have no boundaries or edges — the parallel he draws is that of a sphere which has a finite, measurable surface but has no boundaries (try as we might, we can't fall off the edge of the world: since it is spherical there isn't an edge to fall off). In other words, perhaps there are no boundaries, or beginning or end in terms of time, to the universe. In cautionary tones, Hawking adds, 'I'd like to emphasise that this idea that time and space should be finite without boundary is just a *proposal*.'

The boundary condition of the cosmos is of great concern, simply because scientists are unable to get at it with the tools at their disposal. The laws of physics, as they are known, do not apply in the earliest moments of a creation period, conditions being so different. When a problem cannot be solved one way, the wise scientist tries a different approach. The history of mathematics is filled with attempts to solve equations until one successful method is found, often by trial and error. Hawking's is an attempt to approach the boundary condition of the Universe in a different way. His solution takes us to a different plane — that is, a modified set of dimensions, including imaginary time, in order to describe eventually what happens in the dimensions, real time and real space, with which we are familiar.

Reflecting on the boundary condition problem, Hawking said at the Conference of Astronomical Cosmology held in the Vatican in 1981, 'There ought to be something very special about the boundary conditions of the Universe and what can be more special than the condition that there is no boundary?' This is what he was reaching towards and apparently found in the transformed plane using imaginary time — no beginning, no end. But this endless universe is something that exists in mathematical terms only, as a consequence of the mathematical trick in an imaginary plane. His conclusion therefore holds that 'only if we could picture the universe in terms of imaginary time would there be no singularities [beginning and end]' and 'when one goes back into real time *in which we live*, however, there will still be singularities' (my italics).

Professor Hawking's model is not then, an elegant attempt to re-introduce an Aristotelian, or a Hoylean, eternal universe. It is a device to get around the problems of singularities, those areas where the known laws break down — in particular, the singularity we call creation. The elegance of Hawking's model is not that it leads us to a universe that was without beginning and will be without end; it is that it brings us back, in real time and space, to one which includes singularities — and that is a conclusion lining up nicely with the Second Law of thermodynamics.

CHAPTER SEVEN

A PLURALITY OF SINGULARITIES

JOHN MICHELL WAS A PRIEST. He lived in the eighteenth century during that period of scientific and intellectual ferment begun by Newton's epoch-making book *Principia Mathematica*. The world was assimilating science and John Michell was part of that world. Like many country parsons, as Rector of Thornhill in Yorkshire — now within the heavily industrialised sector of South Yorkshire in England but then part of a rural landscape — Michell had time to pursue his scientific inclinations. They were wide. He had made contributions to mechanics and seismology, but astronomy is where his fertile mind made the greatest impression.

Using only the laws of Newton's mechanics, Michell pondered the effect of gravity on particles and then, since he thought of light as a series of particles (we call them photons today), of the gravitational effects upon light. 'Let us suppose the particles of light to be attracted as all other bodies ...' he mused.

He was aware that light had a speed at which it travelled and he was also aware that to escape the grasping effect of gravity, any particle must have an 'escape velocity', a speed at which it would overcome the gravitational attraction of its parent body to be free of it. (Before a space shot can get into space for example, it must reach the earth's escape velocity or it will always remain in the earth's gravitational field.) Further, Michell recognised that gravitational force increased as the mass of an object increased. He therefore concluded that if an object was massive, yet dense enough for all its mass to be concentrated in a very small volume, so that its gravity was suitably high, then it could impose an escape velocity greater than the velocity of light. In such a circumstance,

Michell concluded that 'all light emitted from such a body would be made to return to it'. No light could escape the body, therefore no one could see it.

Thus, in 1784, the concept of the black hole was born. It didn't have that name then — in fact, it wasn't until 1968 that a physicist, John Wheeler, invented the title. It didn't even have the support of Einstein's general theory of relativity — that wasn't to come for a further 132 years — yet, although inferred using Newton's theory, it could only be predicted mathematically using Einstein's, of which it was a logical outcome.

Michell was not alone in the eighteenth century in proposing black holes. A few years later, the Marquis Pierre-Simon de Laplace — we don't know if he was aware of Michell's thinking — was proposing that 'the attractive force of a heavenly body could be so large that light could not flow out of it'.

What then is the nature of a black hole? Rather like a cosmological Pacman, it gobbles up everything, almost, that comes into its arena of influence. Such is its attractive force that every-thing from particles to planets or suns can be pulled in by its gravity. Just as there is a point of no return for a canoeist upstream of a waterfall on a river, so too for material coming under the influence of a black hole. That point is known as the event horizon and anything crossing it can never again escape. As the canoeist is doomed to go over the waterfall, so too the particle crossing the event horizon is constrained eventually to go to the centre of the black hole where an unknown fate awaits it. Crossing the event horizon on the inward trip is simple — the gravitational attraction of the black hole makes this so — but the crossing cannot be made in the other direction. What goes into a black hole stays there and, because no information relating to the contents of a black hole can re-emerge, the outside observer cannot establish what a black hole contains without himself entering. The picture is well illustrated by the cartoon of the pilot of a space-ship radioing base with the news of his pioneering progress, the first ever, towards a black hole: 'Hello, Mission Control: I'm approaching the black hole now — it's getting closer — I can't yet see what is inside — I'm entering it now — good heavens, it's full of odd socks!'

The story is, however, flawed. The gravity field through which the pilot would necessarily pass would be so great that he and his spaceship would, in all likelihood, be torn apart. Even if he held together, the message reporting the contents of the black hole could never get back across the event horizon. For the tidy minded, it should also be noted that the pilot would never be able to rematch the socks — unless their partners were also sent into the hole.

Since mass, energy and all information is lost in a black hole, we can conclude that entropy also gathers there. In fact, in examining their thermodynamic properties it has been shown that the size of black holes is directly related to the entropy they contain.

How might black holes come into existence? There are four universal forces that control the normal pattern of events in the cosmos and maintain the delicate balance we discover to be involved — the strong nuclear force, the weak nuclear force, the electro-magnetic force and the gravitational force. We shall examine these in more detail in chapter 8. For the moment it is sufficient to say that the first three can dissipate, leaving in a wornout situation only the gravitational force. With nothing to balance this force, a region of the universe could collapse upon itself forming the very dense, very massive conditions necessary for establishing a black hole. It is suggested that there are several ways in which a black hole can be formed, but once it is in existence, there would be no way of finding out which route had been travelled for the formation of any particular black hole.

It is for this reason that black holes, should they exist, would present an inscrutable face to the investigator. If they were able to look like anything, they would all look alike, their contents and history of information having been lost. They might vary in size and they could spin at different rates, but their nature dictates that their family resemblance would be overwhelming.

Of special interest to us though, is an important characteristic of all black holes: according to their mathematics, every one has at its centre a singularity. This means that because of the immense gravitational forces at work there is a spacetime warp — remember the picture we drew earlier of a person's feet on a trampoline — of such great magnitude, that space and time cease to be. If it exists, the centre of a black hole can be described as a cul-de-sac in the universe. In rather more mathematical terms it is known as a boundary of the universe in spacetime [Fig 7.1].

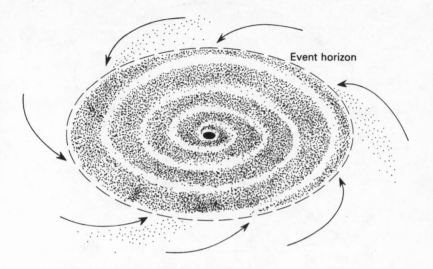

Fig 7.1 A Black Hole
Nobody knows what a black hole looks like. This picture gives the impression of matter being attracted by an immense gravitational field and passing an event horizon, through which it cannot return.

Because of the imponderable conditions at the centre of a black hole, it has become the focus of all sorts of bizarre ideas that belong, not to the realm of science, but that of science fiction. It has been proposed that in passing through a black hole it might be possible to emerge at a different place in the universe, at a different moment in history, or that a black hole is a connecting passage to other universes in which we might pop up like rabbits emerging from their burrows. Such suggestions are, to say the least, fanciful.

We have noted that a singularity is where all the known laws of the universe no longer apply: although we can get close to it, we cannot reach this point meaningfully with the mathematical tools at our disposal. But that doesn't mean that such a point does not exist. One thing we can say about singularities, though, is that just as black holes have similar characteristics, there seems to be no way of telling one singularity from another. Since it is a singularity, though, the centre of a black hole has similarities with another

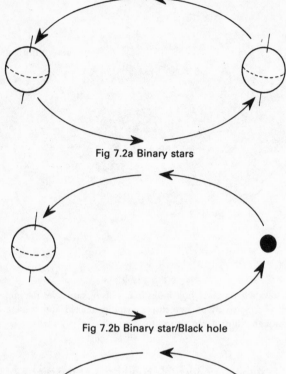

Fig 7.2a Binary stars

Fig 7.2b Binary star/Black hole

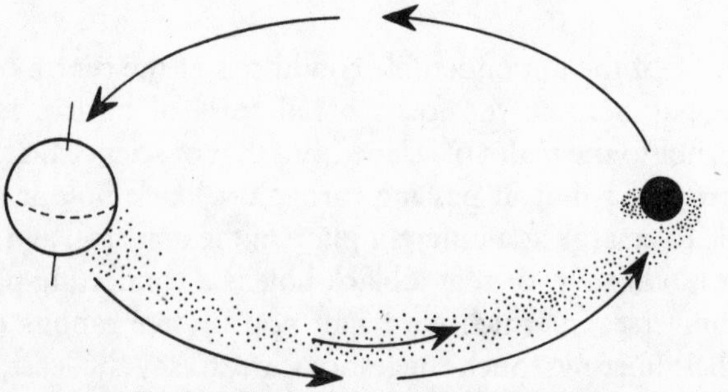

Fig 7.2c Black hole cannibalising a star

Fig 7.2 Binary Systems

A binary star system is drawn schematically in fig 7.2a — the two bodies rotating about each other, held by the gravitational force of the partner. In fig 7.2b, one of the stars has been replaced by a black hole, but the mechanics of the system remain the same. Since a black hole cannot be seen, the rotation of the visible star becomes the evidence for the black hole. It is reckoned that a black hole can suck matter from its partner star (fig 7.2c) and this emits X-rays which may be detected in the vicinity of the earth.

singularity, defining the edge of spacetime in the history of the universe — its birth.

* * *

Black holes present an overwhelming problem to experimental researchers: if, by definition, they can't be seen, how can their existence be proved? This was a problem addressed by Michell who suggested one possible solution, familiar to us all — if we can't see the object, we look for its effect. In the same way, we judge the existence of wind by the result it has on leaves and debris in the streets: so we look at the consequence of the wind's presence, not at the wind. Michell suggested that there might be binary stars — these are pairs of stars whose orbits are about each other, pursuing one another in the heavens as the Chinese polarities Yin and Yang after each other's tail [Fig 7.2a] of which one had become a black hole. The black hole could not be seen, but the gravitational effect on its partner would be measurable in the orbit the partner took. In Michell's words, 'If there should really exist in nature any [such] bodies ... which are not naturally luminous ... we could have no information from sight. Yet if any other luminous bodies should happen to revolve about them, we might still perhaps ... from the motion of these revolving bodies, infer [their] existence' [Fig 7.2b].

We know that binary star systems proliferate in the universe, so it is not impossible to consider that, among the many existing, one of a pair of stars may have collapsed into the form of a black hole while the other retains its starlike characteristics. Each would still circulate the other, locked in a gravity-generated dance. It would be the pattern of movement of the visible star that would give the clue that it had an invisible partner.

Since then, other suggestions of how a black hole might be detected have been made. In a binary star relationship, the black hole would, because of its enormous gravitational attraction, act as a parasite of its partner, sucking material from it [Fig 7.2c] until nothing was left of the star and a bloated black hole was condemned to a lonely existence. If that was the case, while the material was gravitating towards the black hole it would be likely to emit X-rays, very short wavelength light as used in the medical profession, that could be detected by appropriately placed instruments. Unfortunately for those who might want to search for them, such X-rays, if they exist in the cosmos, are largely filtered out by the upper atmosphere before reaching the earth. (Fortunately for us, the atmospheric filter which stops the X-rays getting to the surface of the earth is good news for our health. A sustained dose of X-rays is highly injurious to health and can provoke cancer. That is why the radiologist stands behind a lead screen in an X-ray examination while the photographs are being taken. In a global sense, the atmosphere is nature's lead screen.)

One or two promising sites for a black hole have, however, been found. The most likely is in the constellation Cygnus, the Swan, and is identified as an X-ray source, Cygnus X-1. A second possibility is in a region called the Large Magellanic Cloud and is known to astronomers as LMC X-3. In November 1985, two astronomers reported measurements made in the galaxy NGC 5548 which indicated that a black hole might be eating a star.

NGC 5548 is about 200 million light years from the earth and is classed as a Seyfert galaxy, that is, one which has a very bright nucleus — named after the astronomer Carl Seyfert. Some think that the bright centre is an indication of the activity that would surround a black hole. It was this brightness, which in the case of NGC 5548 varied with time, that was investigated using spectroscopic methods. Spectroscopy is a science in which the wavelengths included in an emitted light can be used to identify the elements in the light source. It is, in short, an optical finger-printing system.

Between February and June 1984, the light intensity of NGC 5548 increased by 60% when it then displayed the presence of large quantities of helium which had not been there before. That was the clue leading to the supposition that a star was going through its death throes, being devoured by an adjacent black hole.

Further possible places for black holes are thought to be at the centre of galaxies. Our own galaxy, the Milky Way, seems to have something going on at the centre whose signal, while not understood, could be the signature of a black hole. Because of the large amount of material in the disc of the galaxy between us and the centre, a distance of 30,000 light years, it is not currently possible to establish what exactly is going on there. The observation, however, is that at the galactic centre, an object identified as Sgr A* is very bright and compact, but appears to be rather small by stellar dimensions. 'Yet it radiates a lot of luminosity. There are many stellar objects in the galaxy that radiate this amount of energy, but this one is peculiar. None of the others is as compact or as steady.' This was the report of one of the discoverers of the phenomenon. Could this be a signature indicating the presence of a black hole? All that can be said is that the measured characteristics appear to fit those of a black hole if one could exist.

These observations do not, however, provide conclusive proof for the existence of black holes, but they can be regarded as promising indications, although not all astronomers would agree. If these are black holes, though, could there be any others up there? In 1970, a satellite with X-ray detection equipment on board was put into earth orbit. It was discovered that the sky was peppered with X-ray sources! Measurements of this type can only be made of black holes which are in binary star combinations: those that are isolated will have no easily measurable signal by which they can be detected. So, maybe there are black holes liberally filling the universe, they could be everywhere, each one having a singularity into which science cannot reach. If a black hole is a sign of a worn-out bit of universe, then we could be viewing a rather moth-eaten garment in the cosmos.

If they are there, black holes are a mute, invisible testimony to the fact that nature has a way of doing things beyond our capacity to evaluate. And if a black hole, together with its singularity, can be reckoned to be in existence today, we cannot discredit the notion of a beginning to the universe on the basis of its being a singularity in which our mathematics is disarmed. The beginning of the universe is also a boundary in spacetime.

*   *   *

What happens to black holes? It is known that, if they exist, they have a voracious appetite as a result of which they grow. Since nothing can get out of their event horizons, they present the idea of a galactic garbage can into which everything in reach, with all its entropy, falls. In fact, they may be thought of as regions of high entropy, that is, disordered energy.

To Stephen Hawking, the thermodynamics of black holes

presented a problem. Objects with temperature always radiate: the sun radiates, a hotplate radiates, our bodies radiate, so a black hole should radiate. But, by definition, nothing could cross the event horizon of a black hole to leave it, so there appeared to be no way for the radiation to get out and fulfil the laws of thermodynamics.

The conundrum was solved by recognising that in the region outside of the event horizon where the force fields would be intense, quantum theory predicts the possibility of short life particle/anti-particle pairs being created. A total energy balance would be maintained in one of the pair having energy in the normal manner while its partner had the equivalent amount of negative energy. Because of their unstable nature, the pair of particles seek to recombine and then annihilate. If, before re-combination, one of the pair is swallowed into the black hole, the other might be freed to go into space without approaching the event horizon. The energy of that particle represents the radiation energy necessary to fulfil the thermodynamics of the system. This became known as Hawking radiation. Its level is, unfortunately, low enough to resist detection.

If the particle entering the black hole was the one with negative energy, the total energy level within the black hole would decrease, a process which, conceivably, could lead to a diminished size and instability of the black hole with eventual extinction. The extinction would be accompanied by an entropy release into the universe so that, overall, the Second Law of thermodynamics is still being fulfilled, as ever.

We may gather a crumb of comfort from this. It is not inevitable that we, or our part of the universe, will be sucked into a giant black hole digesting us and all else in its path. The one thing of which we can be sure, however, is that whatever the progress of the black hole, or the process of the universe, entropy will continue to increase.

*   *   *

The black hole, since it is so far removed from normal experience, is conceptually weird but it has many intellectually stimulating features: not much may come out of a black hole but it can be guaranteed to be a rich source of PhD topics for post-graduate students at universities! For us, though, there are two features of importance.

If black holes exist, Hawking has shown that they must obey the laws of thermodynamics: the Hawking radiation is the imprimatur of that statement. They are therefore subject to entropy increase in operation just like a steam engine. These universal laws permit no exceptions for anything in the physical universe and it is for this reason that whether a black hole grows or finally expires, it has a legacy of entropy increase in the universe overall — in its life-time, its surface area is an indication of the entropy content: in its death, it will not discharge its accumulated debris, be they old stars or odd socks, back into the universe — all of that will have been reconverted into energy which will radiate to the universe. Entropy will be redistributed.

The second point of importance to us is that if black holes are part of our cosmos, then so are singularities. It would require a remarkable extension of physics as we know it to be able to accommodate singularities within a quantifiable, mathematical framework, but that does not arbitrate against their existence. Their presence would make singularities respectable once more, sharpening our approach to the creation and giving it credence, recognising that it is a spacetime boundary. As with the Loch Ness monster if we ever discover that a black hole exists, we shall have to reassess our thinking about origins.

CHAPTER EIGHT

BEGINNINGS AND ENDINGS

H OW, THEN, DID THE UNIVERSE BEGIN, if it did, and *how* will it end, if it does? Can the basic principles of science help us in making assessments, or are we condemned to an ignorance of our origins and destiny, a darkness relieved only by wild conjecture?

The Second Law of thermodynamics is probably the most powerful piece of legislation in the physical world. It ultimately describes every process we have ever discovered: it is the final Court of Appeal in any dispute relating to actions and procedures, whether they are naturally generated or man-inspired. It draws the conclusion that in our universe there is an overall reduction in order, a loss of available energy that is measured as an increase of entropy. So the available stock of order is being exhausted. Akin to the dying battery of a flashlight, useful energy is being dissipated into entropy after which none remains for use. As Clausius said, 'The entropy of the universe is tending to a maximum.'

Rather like mountaineering, the approach to a maximum can only be from a point of lower entropy. Whichever way the peak is climbed, it is always from a lower altitude [Fig. 8.1]. If a maximum is being approached then a minimum must have existed. If there was no overall reduction en route, a condition of the Second Law, it is an unavoidable fact that the minimum was a beginning. For us to live in a universe in which the Second Law of thermodynamics holds, then, it must be a universe that has a starting point, a creation.

What was the beginning like and how did it happen? Because of the limitations of the physics available, no scientific statement can ultimately be made. And so far as can be judged, the singularity

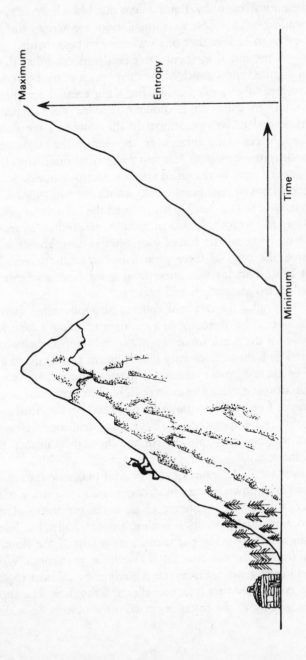

Fig 8.1 Entropy Increase

In ascending a mountain, the mountaineer begins at low altitude and progresses to a high altitude. Similarly, the Second Law of thermodynamics dictates an increase in entropy towards a maximum from a minimum.

that is the spacetime boundary condition generally known as creation will, like all singularities, remain ultimately impenetrable by mathematical ingenuity. But the signs that black holes may exist today, leading us to believe that singularities are here to stay, also encourage us to believe that one was there to begin with.

Although the initial moment can't be described, other than in terms of infinite values, much of the early epoch of the universe, its initial expansion phase, can. The Big Bang created an immense force field from which, it is thought, distilled the five primary forces reckoned to be operational in the whole of the cosmos. These basic forces of the universe are the electric, the magnetic, the weak nuclear, the strong nuclear and the gravitational. The electric and magnetic forces were unified into the electro-magnetic force in the Clerk-Maxwell equations of electro-magnetism to which we made reference in chapter 3. This reduced the number of primary forces from five to four. It also encouraged researchers to seek for ways of unifying all the forces into what is now known as the superforce, the original force present in the creation period. As early as 1850, Faraday was attempting to establish a relationship between electro-magnetism and gravity.

Since they all have different spheres of application, there are difficulties yet to be overcome in a marriage to create a superforce. The action of the weak force causes the decay of particles and is associated with the radioactivity that concerns people living in the vicinity of nuclear power stations. The strong force is the 'glue' to keep sub-atomic particles together: in a nuclear explosion, it is this force we see freed. Electro-magnetic force acts on electrons and to us is useful in the operation of all electrical machinery. Gravity is the force that holds us on the earth and the planets in their paths around the sun.

The four forces (combining electric and magnetic into electro-magnetic) are known to vary in strength and in the scope of their influence. Of particular interest to us is the gravitational force. Between individual particles it is almost insignificant, but because the cosmos has so many particles in it, gravity is the dominant physical force of the universe. But it also varies in strength. While it still operates at great distances, even holding the galaxies together, Newton established that it gets weaker at a rate which he showed to be the square of the distance between the objects. In addition, we know that the overall level of gravity depends on the massiveness of the object creating the gravity field. An object like our sun which contains a lot of matter has a strong gravitational field, and that of a black hole is very strong.

In terms of the physics involved, the early phase of the universe was very complex, a series of concurrent interactive events taking place. The mass of the universe was very confined and the four primary forces may have been united in a massive force-field. Large-scale gravitational fields, such as those predicted around black holes, creating their own spacetime warp, would be equalled or exceeded in strength in this early epoch. We therefore have a picture of matter radiating from an original site, or series of sites, moving at great speed into an expanding spacetime frame unfolding before it as the force-field strength (of enormous proportions) varied.

Because many of these features of the early universe are outside of direct experience, much that is said of this creation period must be conjecture. Nevertheless, confining ourselves only by those theories which are relevant and proved in experience, let us give our thoughts free rein to see where conjecture takes us.

We found in chapter 3 that, in response to the demands of relativity, at high speed a clock would slow down. This is not due to a shortcoming in the design of the clock; rather a fundamental feature of the nature of time. In fact, the example has often been quoted (in slightly modified form) of a hypothetical pair of twins, one staying at home to conserve his energy and lengthen his life, the other an adventurer, willing to trade some of his life for some of life's experiences, going for a trip in a space-ship which travels close to the speed of light. Upon the return of the prodigal, it is discovered that he hasn't been as extravagant with his life as anticipated — he has aged less quickly than his safe, stolid brother. This is because, at the high speed of travel he enjoyed, time went less quickly. He didn't notice it: for him every hour advanced at the rate of an hour per hour in his frame of reference. But for his house-bound brother, the flying brother's hour was stretched according to the clock in the house.

This is usually called time dilation. At low speeds compared with the speed of light, the effect is not noticeable, although, theoretically, a person riding a bicycle is aging less quickly than someone sitting at home. (Where I live, there is a good chance that the cyclist might be knocked off his bicycle by a passing car, thus ceasing to age altogether.) As the speed of light is approached, the time dilation begins to be noticed: at 10% of the speed of light, the change of time measured while moving to that while stationary, the time dilation, is ½%, at 50% it is 15%, at 90% it is 130%, over double. But if the speed is only 1 kilometre per second less than the speed of light, a speed to which protons can be accelerated in modern research equipment, the time dilation becomes 20,000 to 1. That means that where a proton travelling at this speed might experience say, one minute of elapsed time, an outside observer would measure an elapsed time of 137·5 days, a period of about four-and-a-half months!

Relativity also has something to say about the effect of gravity fields upon time. The greater the gravitational field, the greater the time warp or time dilation. Newton has shown that a gravitational field reduces in strength with distance from an object, so we can presume that the greater our altitude above the earth, the faster time will fly. Our working day would then pass more quickly in an office at the top of a high-rise building, but it is not worth the effort of having the office there for that reason: the effect is so small.

In a very high-gravity field, though, the slowing down of time becomes noticeable. Recalling our spaceship pilot entering the black hole, the message he would have communicated to Mission Control before the cut-off point at the event horizon, would have been subject to this time warp. Although to him his speech would have been normal, Mission Control would have heard a progressive frequency drop in his voice: it would have got lower and sl..ow..er as he approached the black hole. The effect of time dilation due to increased gravity is the same as that due to high speed. Time has therefore lost its absolute quality: its value depends upon the frame of reference in which it is quoted.

During the creation period, the effects of both gravity and speed are likely to have been in play, resulting in significant values of time dilation.

*   *   *

How old is the universe?

There are two extreme views that appear to be totally incompatible. Measurement of the total extent of the universe, supported by other evidence, suggests that the moment of creation was 15 billion years ago. Within this framework the age of our galaxy is 10 to 15 billion years and the age of our solar system is about 4·6 billion years. At the other extreme, the calculations of Bishop Ussher, an Irish clergyman who attempted to add up times recorded in the Bible, made an estimate for the elapsed time from creation of about 6,000 years. Such figures become a stumbling block for those of one arithmetic to recognise any good thing in those of another.

But time does not have an absolute quality; it depends upon the frame of reference in which it is quoted. What could be inferred in this instance? We, as observers, view the creation event and subsequent history in a detached sort of way from our frame of reference, outside of this history, since we are at the end of it. Our measurements give us a possible age for the universe of 15 billion years. In the frame of reference of the creation event there was no observer — except, perhaps, a Creator. Because he would have been there before creation, he would, of course, have to be God. Let us assume that, since he was at work in it he recorded the events of creation as he moved in the framework of the creation process — a different time frame. Then let us suppose that he filed his report with a scribe who is resident in our framework. We have noted that the time dilation effect due to speed alone can be 20,000 to 1. When we have taken into account the contribution due to gravitational time warp, this factor is increased further. A convergence begins between the two extreme ages cited, 15 billion years and 6,000 years.

Is this what happened? I don't know: the free rein of conjecture can take us anywhere. But this shows that we must not build a set of dogmas on the assumption that time has the absolute quality inferred by the Newtonian system. Nor must we be totally dismissive of somebody else's arithmetic.

We find that it is not necessary to be a supporter of Bishop Ussher's arithmetic to see that, because of the fundamental contribution Einstein made to science in the theory of relativity, there can be a degree of reconciliation between the measurements of the experimental astronomer and the Bishop. We only need to assume Einstein to be believable and the two frames of reference to exist. If our inclination is towards one particular length of epoch from creation — and that is usually the case — it is not automatically necessary that we must reject the other. Astonishingly, Einstein the Jew has unconsciously given credence, from a scientific perspective, to a set of Jewish writings which are part of what we call the Bible!

*   *   *

'Nature abhors a vacuum' declared François Rabelais. Physicists today tend to agree with Rabelais when viewing the vacuum that separates the galaxies in space. Is it really a vacuum?

Aristotle had filled space with a series of concentric crystalline spheres which were finally dispensed with by the time of Copernicus. The resulting vacuum was filled by René Descartes, the French mathematician who supplied the whole of space with a complex pattern of swirling vortices. Their job was to support and propel the planets in their paths, beyond which further vortices took care of the stars. An engraving in the Bibliothèque Nationale in Paris shows these formations of vortices among which, like flowers in a garden overgrown with weeds, is hidden our planetary system. It is entitled 'The World, According to the Copernican Hypothesis'. With a true sense of political acumen it carries the footnote, 'at the moment of the birth of Louis the Great, the 5 of September at 11 hours and 30 minutes in the morning, 1638'.

Newton didn't need Descartes' vortices or the patronage of Louis the Great for his system: gravity did the job of supporting and propelling the planets, so once more a vacuum prevailed in space.

That was not to remain the case. Particle physicists have been busily filling space once more. The stream of photons from the sun occupies the space between us and it, bringing light to the surface of the earth. Gravitons, gravity's messenger particles which are equivalent to the photon, fill space with the news that we are surrounded with bodies, each of which makes some attractive claim on us. But quantum mechanics, bringing many novel ideas with it, also brings the principle of spontaneous creation of particle/anti-particle pairs. It is this quantum event that results in Hawking radiation from the vicinity of a black hole. Quantum theory postulates the creation of very short life particle/anti-particle pairs, immediately seeking each other out for mutual annihilation, starting from nothing and finishing in nothing. From being a void, space has thus become a seething activity: the picture of a vacuum has been dispensed with again.

There are consequences. The creation of a particle pair appears to be an event without a cause, random — but repeatable. Theoretically, other particles can similarly be created out of nothing if the conditions are right. Was there a right condition for an initial creative event from nothing to signal the creation moment of the universe? Quantum theory might support such an idea. But the thought of an event without a cause is foreign to people brought up on a diet of Newtonian mechanics in which every action had a reaction, thus every event had a cause. These people are in good company. A no-cause event was also repugnant to Einstein and of these consequences of quantum theory he made his often quoted remark, 'God does not play dice.' Einstein was convinced that, even if science could not isolate the cause of a quantum event, beyond its probability, there was a further level of understanding from which its occurrence could be dictated. Ever since Newton had enshrined them in his mechanical laws, there were principles demanding that relationship.

If we are to take Einstein at face value, he was admitting that causes unverifiable by scientific method could result in scientifically measured events. Even though he might not be able to find that level of description for the cause, it was there.

Applying that principle, we must conclude that whether it was a quantum phenomenon or a Big Bang doesn't matter. The event of creation which we can verify in scientific terms had an initial cause — maybe recognisable at a level of understanding beyond scientific reach. Like Einstein, we are driven to the conclusion that God does not play dice. Background radiation of very low intensity but which is highly uniform in all directions is what I have called 'the smoking gun' in chapter 1. The gun needed a finger to pull the trigger. The finger belonged to someone who did not reveal himself directly through quantum mechanics. By the nature of quantum mechanics, though, he replaced the reductionism of Newton and Laplace's mechanical world which did not need a God with one that could not depend on the precision of a set of laws from which all things could be predicted. To that thought we shall return in chapter 10.

Stephen Hawking makes the point that 'Aristotle and most other Greek philosophers did not like the idea of a creation because it smacked too much of divine intervention'. With the argument we have fielded, we must concur with the Greek philosophers: creation does smack of divine intervention. In fact, it is difficult to see how we can avoid it. There is no shortage of those who have tried, but none has yet managed to get around the Second Law and its consequences: that would smack of too little scientific intervention!

*   *   *

The great power of the Second Law is its universally predictive quality. Other laws are, of course, used for prediction, for without that capacity they couldn't be classed as laws. Their predictions depend upon the initial conditions and the set of constraints under which they operate. The Second Law, however, requires no initial conditions to be specified, nor do the process or the operational constraints need to be defined in order to determine the general consequences. The outcome is always an increase of entropy. And since it is the only law that defines the direction of time, the time arrow, it is certain that the entropy increases with time.

We have used this law in determining that the universe had a beginning, creation. Even though the tools of the physicist are unable to break into the secrets of the first moment, we can conclude that it initiated a period of low, but increasing entropy. From the central principle of the Second Law we can conclude that the accuracy of any conjecture, calculation or retrospective assessment about the physics and development of the universe is not important in determining the direction of the universe's advance. Entropy increases whether galaxies are distilled from clouds of gas or digested by black holes. Increasing entropy is therefore taking the universe towards a final end: if the Second Law makes a beginning essential, it makes an end inevitable.

What can be said about the end of the universe? *How* will it end?

Since the time of Hubble's measurements of red shift in the galactic lights, we have known that ours is an expanding universe. Evidence is that the expansion is just above the critical rate beneath which, at some time in the future, gravitational effects would become dominant, reversing the direction of movement. If that is the case, energy will be progressively dissipated as entropy into an increasing cosmic volume — a low temperature random energy to add to the background radiation of the universe, the vestigial consequence of the Big Bang. With the death of our own sun as its energy is exhausted, temperature on the earth will get lower as heat is radiated out to space. Eventually the earth's temperature will be the same as the cosmic background temperature. We have examined this briefly in chapter 5 and discovered a low temperature heat death. When the entropy of the cosmic system reaches its maximum, there will no longer be an arrow of entropy. The intimate relationship between entropy and time that we explored in chapter 5 dictates that there will similarly be no arrow of time. Time will have ceased.

What if the gravitational effects in the universe do eventually take complete charge? The universe will bounce back so that explosion becomes implosion and coalesces into the tight ball from which it is reckoned it initially grew. The ball will not be the same as before, though. Since entropy is not symmetrical in its application, the ball of mass following creation was necessarily in an orderly, smooth condition — low entropy, but that at the final moment it will be in a state of disorder — high entropy.

Time would once more draw to a close, the massive gravitational force-field creating a spacetime warp of such proportions that a boundary condition would result as at the creation or in a black hole. For us, there would have been a heat death of high temperature.

So far as the earth is concerned, another potential form of heat death lurking in the wings is that due to the greenhouse effect. We know that the results of industrialisation on the earth are leading to heat, as entropy, being trapped in the atmosphere by 'greenhouse gases'. It is conceivable that a run-away condition could result. Some prophets of doom see the earth of tomorrow rather like that of Venus today — a planet with a hostile atmosphere locking heat into its sphere so that surface temperatures are extremely high. If that was to happen to the earth, the universe would hardly notice. The overall processes would continue either to an eventual expanded, low-temperature state or to a recollapsed ball.

Although he offers a modification in adding the possible effects of quantum principles, Stephen Hawking uses the General Theory of Relativity to highlight conditions at the beginning and ending of the universe.

> According to the General Theory of Relativity there must have been a state of infinite density in the past, the Big Bang which would have been an effective beginning of time. Similarly, if the whole Universe recollapsed, there must be another state of infinite density in the future, the Big Crunch, which would be an end of time. Even if the whole Universe did not recollapse, there would be singularities in any localised regions that collapsed to form black holes. These singularities would be an end of time for anyone who fell into a black hole. At the Big Bang and other singularities, all the laws would have broken down, so God would have complete freedom to choose what happened and how the Universe began.

God controls the singularities.

That brings us to a further possible terminal point for the universe that we can't ignore. Since we have no means of establishing the conditions that caused the universe to start, we have to consider the possibility that we have no means of actually predicting how it will end. Put another way, we don't know what motivated the finger to pull the trigger of the gun called creation, starting everything to work: how can we say that we might predict when the finger will press the button to stop it all working? As the God we postulate controls the singularities, we may conclude that he has complete freedom to choose what has happened and what will happen.

CHAPTER NINE

THE PATTERN OF CHAOS

IN CROSSING A HEATH, suppose I pitched my foot against a stone and were asked how the stone came to be there; I might possibly answer that, for anything I knew to the contrary, it had lain there for ever: nor would it perhaps be very easy to show the absurdity of this answer. But supposing I had found a watch upon the ground and it should be enquired how the watch happened to be in that place; I should hardly think of the answer which I had before given, that for anything I knew, the watch might always have been there. Yet why should not this answer serve for the watch as well as for the stone?

With these words, written in 1802, William Paley introduced his book *Natural Theology*. It was, over many years, to become compulsory reading for students going up to Cambridge and has remained in publication since.

Paley was laying out the Design Argument which brought him to the conclusion that 'there cannot be design without a designer, contrivance without a contriver, order without choice, arrangement without anything capable of arranging'. Whether Paley knew of Robert Boyle, whose work led to one of the fundamental laws of thermodynamics, Boyle's Law, we cannot be sure. Boyle had already used the watch analogy in developing his own argument for a mechanical world. He had evidently been influenced by Newton's *Principia* and saw a similarity between the workings of the universe and those of a watch. The analogy has been used since then by many who stand either for, or against, the Design Argument.

Is there an identifiable pattern, an arrangement in the cosmos? Is it contrived or is it just one of those accidents that can occur? What are the implications and how will they help us to discover the *why* that goes beyond the *how* of the universe?

To attempt an answer, let us look at some of the features of the cosmos which are either so familiar or so deeply part of its fabric that we do not normally question them.

In the cosmological model that harmonises with the Second Law — a beginning at a point in time — we have found that the universe had the characteristic of increasing entropy and, in chapter 8, concluded that this entropy principle brought about a minimum entropy at the creation. That leaves us with a question however: unless it knew what was to come, why was the creation a time of minimum entropy?

The Second Law can be interpreted in a statistical manner, that is, in terms of the probability of an event. In chapter 5, we used the example of a container with red and blue liquid mixing to produce purple liquid. The condition of the separated red and blue particles was associated with low entropy and that of the mixed particles, a purple liquid, with high entropy. It is sometimes argued that, in the random mixing process that normally brings about the purple result, it is not impossible for the red particles to happen to be at one end of the container and the blue at the other producing a new, low entropy condition. We will examine that possibility later, but for the moment, note that there are only two conditions allowing the red and blue to be separate, one with the red at one end and, alternatively, at the other end of the container, the blue following suit. But there are innumerable particle mixtures that give purple, so we can say that the purple is more probable than the separate red and blue pattern. In terms of entropy we say that high entropy is more probable than low entropy, or disorder more likely than order. The Second Law states that all systems tend towards disorder (or, in our case, purple). High entropy is therefore a likely, and low entropy an unlikely, situation.

It is evident that if many more disordered than ordered states are possible and we apply the argument to creation, a disordered state was more likely than an ordered one at the beginning. Stephen Hawking put this as a question in *A Brief History of Time*: 'Why should the Universe be in a state of high order at one end of time, the end we call the past? Why is it not in a state of disorder at all times? After all, this might seem more probable.' William Paley's answer is that it is the sign of a contrivance behind which there is a contriver. In this book we have approached this point from a different perspective. In chapter 5 we saw that man is the creature of an entropy-increasing world outside of which he wouldn't be able properly to employ his faculties of memory or experience: homo sapiens — thinking man — could not be. So, low entropy is a necessary starting point for a universe that will be occupied, at some time, by man. If there is a contriver for this universe — and the improbability of a low entropy beginning points to one — then his contrivance included the possibility of man's existence.

But there are other aspects of the cosmos that tell a similar story of contrivance. In chapter 8 we outlined the four forces comprising the force system of the universe. Cosmologists have concluded that in the first few moments of a Big Bang they would have been united in a superforce before distilling into their separate identities. Not only do they have different jobs to do, each one has a value which is precisely defined and these values vary enormously in strength. 'Yet this enormous and exact difference is of crucial importance — a matter literally of life and death. Nearly all modern physicists find such facts so striking that they are forced to wonder aloud philosophically or even theologically,' concluded Mark Doughty, an academic from Montreal in Canada, writing in *The Tablet* in October 1988.

Certainly, these fundamental constants of nature appear to be carefully set. John Barrow and Frank Tipler, academics from Sussex in England and New Orleans in the United States of America respectively, and authors of *The Anthropic Cosmological Principle*, comment on the vital quality of these values, noting that 'most perturbations of the fundamental constants of nature away from their actual numerical values lead to model worlds that are still-born, unable to generate observers and become cognizable. Usually, they allow neither nuclei, atoms nor stars to exist.' Emphasising how critical such changes would be, they use as an example a simple system consisting of deuterium (a proton, a neutron and an electron) which is an isotope of hydrogen (that is, with the same chemical character as hydrogen but with the addition of a neutron in its atomic make-up) and diproton (a proton and a proton).

The existence of deuterium and the non-existence of the diproton therefore hinge precariously on the precise strength of the nuclear force. If the strong interaction were a little stronger the diproton would be a stable bound state with catastrophic consequences — all the hydrogen in the Universe would have burnt to diproton during the early stages of the Big Bang and no hydrogen or long-lived stable stars would exist today. If the diproton existed, we would not! Also if the nuclear force were a little weaker ... the key link in the nucleosynthesis would be removed. Elements heavier than hydrogen would not form.

The consequences are profound. If the formation of simple substances is critically associated with precise values of the fundamental constants of nature, then the formation of anything more complex is even more precarious. Without hydrogen, there is no building block for the universe. The smallest deviation of the forces necessary to bind the proton and electron that constitute hydrogen are therefore of immeasurable importance to us.

To underline how essential it was for the magnitude of these forces to be exactly correct, Barrow and Tipler add:

> If the relative strengths of the nuclear and electro-magnetic forces were to be slightly different then carbon atoms could not exist in nature and human physicists would not have evolved [neither would human non-physicists who, strangely, are made of the same stuff]. Likewise many of the global properties of the Universe ... must be found to lie within a very narrow range if cosmic conditions are to allow carbon-based life to arise.

Quoting Brandon Carter an astrophysicist, in his book *Super-force*, physicist Paul Davies sees 'an almost unbelievable delicacy in the balance between gravity and electro-magnetism within a star. Calculations show that changes in the strength of either force by only one part in 10^{40} [that is, one part in 10 with 40 zeros after it] would spell catastrophe for stars like the sun.'

Professor Hawking notes 'the remarkable fact that the values of these numbers seem to have been very finely adjusted to make possible the development of life'. In the words of Fred Hoyle, 'The laws of nuclear physics have been deliberately designed with regard to the consequences they produce inside stars. If this is so, apparently random quirks have become part of a deep-laid scheme.' He called creation a 'put-up job'!

*   *   *

The Big Bang is a useful and evocative title for the beginning of the cosmos. Whether it was a bang, a click or a thud is of no consequence. The name gives the impression, which is intended, of a moment of initiation. It happens that we can't get into it with our physics but, just as the consequences of an explosion give forensic experts many details about the explosion, so too there is much that can be deduced from the event of the Big Bang by the remains which are left for examination.

The judgement that Paul Davies passes on it in *Superforce* is that:

> the explosive vigour of the Universe is matched with almost unbelievable accuracy to its gravitating power. The Big Bang was not, evidently, any old bang, but an explosion of exquisitely arranged magnitude. In the traditional version of the Big Bang we are asked to accept not only that it happened, but that it happened in an exceedingly contrived fashion. The initial conditions had to be very special indeed.... It was a highly orchestrated explosion, a simultaneous burst of exactly uniform vigour everywhere and in every direction.

The results are these. The background radiation of the universe, the 'smoking gun' of chapter 1, is of uniform intensity in every direction, suggesting a high degree of uniformity in the initial event leading to the expansion. The expansion of the universe, discovered by Hubble and noted in chapter 6, appears to be precisely set so that it neither runs away in an accelerating manner, resulting in a universe long since dissipated, nor will the expansion give way to recompression for a final Big Crunch (an end will come by means other than recompression). In addition, just enough non-uniformity (like the graininess in granary bread) was included in the original chemistry to allow galaxies to distil and form. With less non-uniformity we could conceive a homogenous cosmos, a thin soup swirling through space. More non-uniformity and maybe the initial entropy would have been too high for a development to the universe we recognise.

*   *   *

The precision in the basic fabric of the cosmos, examined in isolation, bespeaks a mechanical universe, constructed with consummate skill, set going and left to operate in its appointed and perfect manner. Newtonian physics, although lacking the ability to account for the effects of the speed of light, nevertheless pointed the way to a determinism that would describe, in every detail, the future. This was certainly the vision of Laplace: 'All the effects of nature are only the mathematical consequences of a small number of immutable laws.' But closer examination of the workings of our system show that this is not quite the case.

Thursday 4th October, 1582, was an unusual day for it was followed by Friday 15th October, 1582 — the day that the Julian calendar gave way to the Gregorian calendar. This was a recognition that the solar system didn't work exactly as the arithmetic preferred. Perhaps it was because some people seriously felt that they had been robbed of eleven days of their lives (riots were reported) that the new calendar was a little while in being accepted — in Russia it was adopted in 1917 and in Japan it still hasn't been adopted — but it showed that a more rigorous accountancy needed to be made of the earth's rotation if errors were not to be such that eventually, midsummer day was not to fall in the middle of winter. The rules of leap year provided a predictable regulatory pattern. But the accuracy of time measurement has improved. Today atomic clocks are of such quality that it is feasible for leap seconds to be employed in maintaining time in step with the position and rotation of the earth in its path. While leap years are absolutely predictable, leap seconds are not. Within the system whose mechanics can be precisely described, the leap second bears testimony that there are unpredictable changes. Why?

Our calculations are based on an earth which is a solid body in rotation. But it isn't. There are tidal systems which wash their way around, a result of the moon's gravitational pull. In addition, the solid surface of the earth is not fixed, but is made up of huge slowly moving plates comprising flexible formations which themselves bend under the pressures of movement and through the moon's compelling presence. The result is that, although the mechanics are well known by any senior school pupil, we have no means of making an ultimately accurate statement of what happens.

It is a curious thing to note that these perturbations, small as they may be, are destabilising to the solar system which creates them and of which they are part. And every engineer knows that perturbations when damped, die away completely, but undamped

Fig 9.1 Blade-tip Wakes
This remarkable photograph shows the activity at the tip of an aerodynamic blade, a beautiful pattern of turbulence which speaks of an increase of entropy.

tend to grow to a point at which a system destabilises. These perturbations have not died away. And yet the solar system, revolving for, it is thought, 4·6 billion years, still operates in a cyclic sort of way. It has not disintegrated, its component planets having wandered into space, untethered from the sun and each other. Although we can measure the effects of the destabilising forces, the problem of the stability of the solar system remains unsolved.

The growth of entropy provides further evidence of phenomena which can be precisely stipulated but not precisely described. The wake patterns from an aircraft are not normally seen by the observer: the flow has to be seeded in some manner to make it visible. When they can be seen, however, the patterns have remarkable beauty [Figs 9.1, 2]. The detailed mathematics of fluid mechanics are known and general predictions may be made of the losses associated with the wakes, their direction of movement, their spread and decay, but their detailed structure still defies accurate description.

For a period I focused on research in the field of unsteady fluid flows, the behaviour of airflows when subject to conditions that varied rapidly with time. When I began, no measurement had ever been made of the behaviour of a series of aerofoil sections (rather like a row of aircraft wings) in gusting situations, such as we knew were encountered in aero-gas turbine compressors. My team developed an instrumentation system to explore the phenomenon. Without the benefit of equipment now available we used what we could — even conscripting the use of those tiny electric motors used in slot-racing cars (motor burn-out was a regular occurrence and a colleague was deputed to the local toy shop to buy replacements — it was widely rumoured that we had the largest slot-racing circuit in the world!), but finally the measurements were successfully made. They were amazing, and in a film made to illustrate what was happening, they had a remarkable effect on the delegates of a scientific conference on Unsteady Fluid Mechanics in the United States. But here's the rub: the sinuously moving lines were describing, in the film, the detailed behaviour of air merely being obedient to quite basic laws of motion and entropy growth, but we couldn't predict their details at all, much less predict them accurately. I was a little peeved to discover, though, that in overall terms my results agreed very precisely with a prediction made by two researchers in 1935, forty years before my work was published! Even with a forty-year background of knowledge, we still couldn't make an accurate detailed prediction of what we were measuring.

One of the fascinating things about wakes, like those from aeroplanes and ships, is that the detailed picture we see is much the same, however it is magnified. Within the structure there appears to be an almost identical structure repeated. This is broadly the definition of a fractal, a strange and alluring series of images that can be found in nature but also generated on computers. Fractals can be interpreted as a sign of entropy. The coastline of a country is a fractal: whether it is observed from a spaceship, from an aeroplane, from standing on it or through a magnifying glass, the interface between the sea and the land has much the same crenellated pattern. Computer-generated pictures of fractals are quite astonishing. The patterns often look as if they should adorn a piece of silk as a design, but delving into part of a

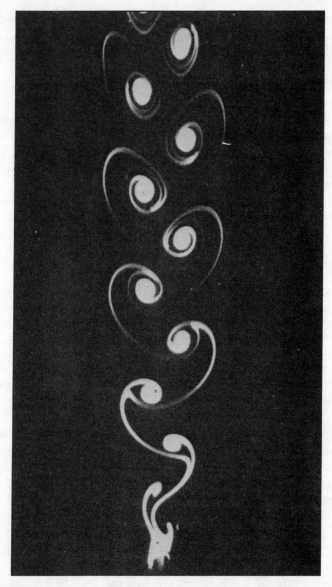

Fig 9.2 Wakes from Wings
Behind a wing, or any section — a circular cylinder was used here — there is a shedding of vorticity which can have a beautiful structure as indicated here. An aeroplane is continually making patterns such as those shown here, contributing to increased entropy.

pattern produces a further similar pattern. Although we can evaluate them using quite simple equations, they are a source of continual amazement and few would be brave enough to predict their shape without the calculation to help [Fig 9.3].

Of course, we don't need to consider esoteric subjects, leap seconds, the solar system stability or fractals to recognise the difficulty in making predictions in what should be a deterministic situation. The fluid mechanics of low-speed air and air/water vapour mixtures is well documented and there is little to be learned of the mathematics of these processes, yet weather forecasting is always liable to be wrong.

It is small wonder that, by the end of his life, Laplace had changed his reductionist philosophy of determinism. His last words were, 'What we know is not much: what we do not know is immense.'

William Paley's observation was:

> So, then, the watch in motion establishes to the observer two conclusions. One, that thought, contrivance and design have been employed in the forming, proportioning and arranging of its parts; and that whoever or wherever he be, or where, such a contriver there is, or was. The other; that force, or power, distinct from mechanism, is at this present time acting upon it. If I saw a hand-mill even at rest, I should see a contrivance: but if I saw it grinding, I should be assured that a hand was at the windlass, though in another room. It is the same in nature.

*   *   *

It seems strange that a universe created with such an ordered and delicate balance in its chemistry, biology, physics and mechanics should be dominated by the Second Law of thermodynamics, dedicated to replacing order with disorder. We have described the consequences of the Second Law, entropy, as a measure of the chaos in a system, increasing towards a maximum. But the result of the intrusion of entropy into this beautiful picture is not simply to create a cosmic bedlam of disorder and chaos. Chaos can have pattern. The wakes from an aircraft are the bearers of entropy. The energy lost to the wakes eventually dissipates into the atmosphere, but in the meanwhile the entropy is locked up in the graceful curves of the vortices shed from the wings of the aeroplane. The vortices contain energy that can no longer be gainfully employed in the process of driving the aircraft through the air.

Fig 9.3 Fractals
Note how the patterns are always coherent and eventually reproduce, irrespective of the degree of magnification.

Similarly, the patterns of my unsteady flow experiments, whose descriptive diagrams gave the impression of water plants moving gracefully in the varying currents of the sea, were signs of entropy, energy lost for ever from the process in my investigations. Fractals, too, contain pattern, design.

We must differentiate between the patterns that are created by entropy growth and those that must be destroyed by it. The red and blue particles in our container were initially in a pattern — red at one end and blue at the other. We equated the growth of entropy with mixing the constituents into purple — the pattern broke down. I have also mentioned the possibility of the random walk of the particles in their container reproducing the original condition of separated red and blue. It is sometimes argued that since this could happen, one day it will. It is even concluded from this that the Second Law does not always hold. The monkey sitting at the typewriter and reproducing a Shakespearian sonnet without fault is a parallel. I might reject the monkey hypothesis out of pique since I can't sit at a typewriter and type out anything without fault! More important though is the scientific observation of this event. If the monkey sits at the keyboard I am now using, the chances are one in $1 \cdot 5 \times 10^{17}$ (that is one chance in $1 \cdot 5$ with 17 noughts after it) that he will successfully type 'Monkey'. If he presses a key twice a second (about my own speed), works an eight-hour day, a five-day week, takes a well-earned rest for four weeks a year plus national holidays, he will take 12,000,000,000 years to complete his task — around 80% of the reckoned age of the universe! That is the result of a simple statistical calculation (as an exercise, you can calculate how long I took to type this manuscript).

More important than statistics, is the need to trace this literate biped that can put me to shame on my own computer. It seems that he is an absentee temp. He hasn't been found and the reason is this: he is a denial of the Second Law. Random behaviour *could* produce the works of Shakespeare (although Shakespeare would probably be rather annoyed at the thought) but it doesn't.

Where does that leave us?

Our knowledge, which we shuffle into laws to describe what we have seen and make predictions for what we will see, is based on the undeviating course of our experience. Our experience has yet to encounter the marvellous monkey and we have yet to see the red particles migrate to one end of the container leaving the blue to the other — football teams of particulates gathering for instructions from their respective captains. And this is important, 'we have yet to see', for it is a surprising thing to discover that laws cannot in general be proved, only disproved. The fall of a brick to the ground proves that the attractive force of gravity has operated on that particular brick. Reasonably, we say that until we find to the contrary, we will assume that gravity will have the same effect on all bricks, but unless we drop every brick manufactured, the law is not absolutely proved. Nevertheless, we accept it and the law decides the framework of equipment used on building sites.

Similarly with the Second Law of thermodynamics — we accept it until it is seen to be contravened. If the moment comes when it is violated — all the red particles fleeing to one end of the container only because a series of random events has made that journey necessary, we have a problem. The most fundamental law in science is shown to be wrong and the sum total of scientific philosophy, law and structure dependent on the Second Law fall about our ears — like bricks.

Until that time, we continue with the dogma that the Second Law holds, particles do not behave in an exclusive manner and monkeys continue to monkey about as they always have done, leaving higher things to Shakespeare. Particles do not assemble themselves in patterns of lower entropy although entropy can have pattern. The contriver is still in control.

*   *   *

We have then a design, with all the evidence of contrivance and a hand still 'at the windlass', as William Paley perceived the controlling force of the working mechanism. What is behind all this, or, to put it in the form of Stephen Hawking's question, 'Why does the Universe go to all the bother of existing? Is the Unified Theory so compelling that it brings about its own existence? Or does it need a Creator, and, if so, does he have any other effect on the Universe?'

Using the normal astronomical methods of observation and reckoning, we find that the universe is about 15 billion years old. Yet there is not much evidence of man's imprint on earth before, at most, 100,000 years ago — probably less. Philosophers of science sometimes use what is called the Anthropic Principle in determining the relationship between the universe and man. In its briefest form, this principle is a statement that the universe was made for man, not man for the universe. Like most things that people think about for a few minutes, though, the principle is now divided into at least two sub-sections known, respectively, as the Weak Anthropic Principle and the Strong Anthropic Principle. The weak version says that at some time somewhere in the universe there exist regions where life, as we know it, can exist. That we are here is evidence of that. The strong version replaces the 'can' by a 'must' — it is an imperative for the universe.

We can only consider a universe which is finite spatially and in time. An infinite universe, one which has always been here and will always remain, stretching through a spatial infinity with all the universal descriptive parameters varying in every way possible must, at some point, have conditions which encourage the existence of intelligent life, sites suitable for human habitation. In that case any discussion about man's possible place ceases: he is an inevitable product of a set of local conditions which must eventually occur. However, if the infinite series of sets in this infinite universe produces one set of conditions which is conducive to man's existence, a closely related set in that part of an infinite cosmos must encourage different species closely related to man to co-exist — near-man — whose only difference from man would allow for local galactic variations in the climate.

But the everlasting nature of the infinite universe contradicts the Second Law of thermodynamics. To consider this type of universe we must therefore dispense with the Second Law and also anything depending on it, our experience of science and life. The infinite universe is a place where anything we think might happen, can and does. It is the perfect setting for science fiction.

But near-man has yet to be found and, in any case, the universe is only 15 billion light years across — it has finite limits. This dimension is related to its apparent age, 15 billion years, which sets limits, beyond which, in physical terms, there is nothing.

Within this finite universe why has man been around for such a short while? Certainly, the conditions are right for him now and this suggests that they have not always been so. None of us would have fared well in the epoch following a Big Bang or in the subsequent cooling period as the universe expanded to the point necessary for our climate to be right. The size of the universe is, we discover, a condition of man's existence. Today is man's time.

But if man is a creature of chance, an incidental but inevitable product of the seething debris of a cataclysmic explosion, and if all the species on the earth are the result of an unthinking set of chemical reactions, we encounter problems. We should expect evidence of a near-man species suited to an environment immediately prior to ours, yet unable to live in today's. He cannot be a link between an ape and a man which coexist in the current world climate, for in that case he too would coexist, finding this to be a user-friendly climate like those he links, his predecessor and progeny. He must be the product of a climate in which neither man nor ape could live. We have yet to find him.

Nor, in our current environment, do we find a blending of species. Horses of different breeds abound and so do deer, both of which thrive today in this world. But while a horse has no horns and a deer has two, there is no evidence for an in-between species with one horn. The unicorn seems reserved for the pages of children's books. But if different species can develop from a common ancestor, then so could all the in-betweens of these species, resulting in a continuous blending of type from, say, a horse to a deer.

Neither can discrete species be the product of a random selective effect — the law of the jungle. There is nothing selective about predators that would feed on them to eliminate deer with one horn less or horses with one added. Predators are not usually known for being that fussy about their food.

Even within a species, discrete differences are found. Richard Dawkins writes in his book *The Blind Watchmaker* of the adaption of fish to their environment. Vertical fish, wanting to live close to the sea-bed, found it uncomfortable to sit on the knife-edge of their vertical bodies. So they developed into flat fish to make it easier to hug the sea bed. But we have yet to find a continuous range of fish varying in skeletal structure through the diagonal, from vertical to horizontal that would be the necessary transient to validate the story. Without this evidence of the blending of the vertical and the flat varieties I must conclude the story to be fishy!

Unicorns, mermaids, centaurs and ET all have characteristics conducive to survival — probably better than that of man who can't gallop, swim or move with facility through space — but it seems that William Paley's contriver didn't arrange things to be that way. What we are viewing is design, contrivance — not accident, chance.

It was in looking at the remarkable make-up of the ear and the eye in a range of animals that Paley made the general conclusion: 'Wherever we see the marks of contrivance, we are led for its cause to an intelligent creator.'

The more I explore this subject, the greater is the conviction that, setting all else aside and from the scientific viewpoint alone, I see a designer who has contrived the most amazing cosmos whose characteristics are balanced on a knife-edge of improbability, ready to topple off should there not be the corrective hand 'at the windlass'. But it is a cosmos so fashioned that it would be the residence of man whom he would create. Stephen Hawking, examining the uniformity of the initial state of the universe, concluded that, so carefully were things chosen that 'it would be very difficult to explain why the Universe should have begun this way, except as the act of a God who intended to create beings like us'. That is a good, considered view, speaking of an intelligent creator. The *how* begins to direct us towards the *why*.

If the creator intended to create man as part of his grand contrivance, *why* did he do it? And what is the significance of the answer? This is what we shall explore in the next chapter, using the evidence of the men whose evidence shaped our understanding of the cosmos and the physics that makes it work.

CHAPTER TEN

A LESSON FOR OUR TIME

WE HAVE SEEN HOW a knowledge of the universe has grown from Aristotle's concept of crystalline spheres sliding effortlessly around a centre occupied by the earth. There have been two spurs for this. The more obvious is that we want realistic models without error in their predictive ability. But there is a deeper impulse: going beyond the *how* which gives the accurate forecast, is the question *why*? On the assumption that one leads to another, the best model of *how* has become an imperative to get the best answer to *why*. There has been the assumption that a totally satisfactory *how* described in real terms — explaining by realistic scientific laws, calculations by scientific procedures — leads to the real *why*.

The path of discovery has taken us from the very large — the universe, its constituent galaxies and their members, to the very small — sub-atomic particles with short-range nuclear forces and long-range gravitational forces. The reasons why the two sizes, large and small, have been connected in our thinking, goes back to Platonic philosophy. In the *Timaeus*, Plato declared that it was essential to understand the smallest component of the universe in order to understand the universe. In other words, the sum of the parts was beyond comprehension without fully comprehending the parts.

The heroic age of Plato and Aristotle was the fifth century BC. In the two-and-a-half thousand years of scientific endeavour that have followed, have we approached the end of the road? Do all the questions have answers, or, at least, are the answers almost within our grasp?

In the early developments of cosmology and the associated

physics, the errors being addressed were gross. Mars mis-behaved and when one of the most obvious of the lights in the sky refused to agree with the theory that Aristotle had asserted — circular motion dependent on the regular movement of concentric spheres in which the planets were embedded — there was a problem. In retrospect, we see Ptolemy's solution, the earth being displaced slightly from the centre of the universe, as the first step towards its dethronement from a central, important, position in a cosmological system.

But the solution didn't go far enough in meeting the problem. To maintain the doctrine of circular motion, epicycles — and then, epicycles on epicycles — were necessary to make predictions that were even approximately right. What created such trajectories for the planets, Mars in particular, was unimaginable.

There was, then, a very confusing picture left for Copernicus to address. His solution was revolutionary in concept and expression. The new concept can be understood in seeing a letter he received from an adherent of the old system. 'I have always believed that hypotheses are ... the bases of computation,' he was told, 'so that, even if they be false, it is of no consequence, provided they exactly reproduce the phenomena of the motions.' Copernicus had a different approach: he wanted to produce something scientifically realistic, not mathematically convenient, and it was on the basis of his quest for reality that he knew the system of epicycles for planetary motion to be unacceptable. So a revolution resulted, a system centred on the sun, heliocentric, rather than on the earth, geocentric. But it was a revolution to be realised in another generation.

Copernicus, while taking a thoroughly novel approach to the overall geography of what we now call the solar system, was still shackled by circular orbits. It remained for two men, Kepler the mathematician and Galileo the experimental investigator, to un-ravel the mysteries of the planetary orbits and prove the helio-centric system as a reality. Kepler, working with the data from Tycho Brahe's measurements, used brilliant intuition coupled with a doggedness in calculation after calculation to discover, not only the elliptical tracks for the planets to run on, but also the variation of planetary speed around the tracks. Galileo produced the evidence. The moons of Jupiter, the phases of Venus, sunspots all combined to undermine traditionally held Aristotelian views of the cosmos. The surface of our moon and the Milky Way were not what we thought them to be, but, most important, the earth was not the pivot of the universe as Aristotelian tradition had demanded. Realism had triumphed, but at a price. Reality was no longer a direct consequence of feeling and its associated common sense. The observer on the earth didn't feel that he was moving, but the reality of Copernicus said that he was — and at considerable speed.

What was then to follow was described by Alexander Pope in the famous epigram:

> Nature, and Nature's laws lay hid in night,
> God said, 'Let Newton be!' and all was light.

So it was. Out of all that had gone before, Newton created a rationalistic mechanical universe which followed clearly prescribed laws, simply expressed. Mars fell into line, fictitious circles were replaced with the naturally generated shapes of ellipses and everything worked with precision. Cause and effect worked hand in hand in accordance with Galileo's axiom, 'for any one effect there must be a single, true and optimal cause'. The disinterested observer could be forgiven for declaring that the end of physical discovery and of further advance in physics was at hand. Yet, as we have mentioned, Mercury was obstinate enough not to yield to such a beautiful set of propositions as Newton had devised.

Newton's mechanics were extended from scientific statements into philosophical principles in the hands of others. Every sphere of life was eventually touched by the Newtonian philosophy: 'all social facts linked together in necessary bonds eternal, by immutable, inelectable and inevitable laws' which would be obeyed by individuals and governments when once made known to them. Man was now part of the Newtonian mechanism of the universe. He no longer operated as a free agent but was programmed to run along his own particular track. Freedom, the mind and man's response suffered. But so too did man's view of God. In this reductionist world, God wasn't necessary: the very mechanics of the universe, at one time taken as the signature of his hand, were now presented as the proof that he didn't exist.

But the turn of the twentieth century altered this picture. As Alexander Pope was to Newton, so was JC Squire to Einstein. With tongue in cheek and Pope in mind, Squire wrote:

> It did not last: the devil howling, 'Ho!
> Let Einstein be!' restored the status quo.

Einstein destroyed gravity — the glue that held Newton's universe together — mixed space and time into a cocktail that he bent, shaping a new physics whose way had been pointed by Faraday and Clerk-Maxwell. In passing, Mercury was tamed and its trajectory almost agreed with the prediction arising from Einstein's relativity.

Meanwhile, a totally new concept was being carved out by Max Planck; quantum theory, which finally removed all certainty from a hitherto deterministic world. The turn of the twentieth century is therefore normally regarded as the dividing point between classical physics, the mechanistic, and modern physics, that of chance, the probable and the improbable. Certainty was replaced by uncertainty.

Arising from the new physics it was thought that effects no longer needed causes. Therefore the creation was an effect that didn't need a cause, a creator. So just as, to some, a deterministic world left no room for God, the result of a non-deterministic world also meant that there was no place for God. Either way, he was declared to be redundant.

*   *   *

Stephen Hawking, in his inaugural lecture as Lucasian Professor of Mathematics, reported that in the late 1920s Max Born told a group of scientists that 'physics as we know it, will be over in six months'. It wasn't, because the physics which had been emerging also had its casualty, certainty. That is possibly why, in answering the question which was the title of his lecture, 'Is the End in Sight for Theoretical Physics?' Hawking's opinion was only a cautious 'yes'.

After two-and-a-half thousand years, the quest for knowledge has produced much, but many of the fundamentals, reckoned at one time to be fully understood, are now seen not to be clearly established. The old certainties are gone. Atomic particles are found to have structure and hence be divisible. As a result, the elementary particles that form the most basic building brick of the universe have still positively to be identified. Quarks, which are reckoned to be the main constituent of most matter, have a variety of six 'flavours' and three 'colours', as their sub-divisions are known, giving eighteen varieties overall — so there may be a further sub-division at a lower level to find the building block of the quark. The geography of the atom is no longer a miniature of a solar system, electrons in stable well-appointed orbits around a nucleus, but it can't be said exactly what replaces it. The path of particles between two points is not determined uniquely by a force-field but has been replaced by a range of possible routes. The position and velocity of a particle cannot both be determined simultaneously. The creation of particle/anti-particle pairs is a matter of chance, not cause and effect. Protons, always thought to be stable particles, decay. Light has a dual personality, in some ways behaving like waves and in some ways as particles.

On a larger scale, there are also unknowns. Mercury does not quite agree with its predictions, although the error is only about one in two hundred. Other questions remain: how much dark matter is in the universe; how will the universe end, if it does; why is the Hubble Constant for universal expansion up to 100% in error; do black holes exist; what really happens in a black hole; what happens at a singularity and hence happened in the singularity called creation; how did creation occur?

The new physics has raised many questions and the problem is this. Physicists now find it increasingly difficult to identify experiments that will illuminate the theory and answer the questions. And without an interrogation of nature by experiment, theory must always remain theory. Einstein, in his homage to Max Planck, stressed the importance of experimentation: 'Nobody who has really gone deeply into the matter will deny that in practice the world of phenomena uniquely determines the theoretical system.' In his *Discourses Concerning Two New Sciences*, Galileo wrote of 'mathematical demonstrations [being] applied to natural phenomena. The principles thus established by well-chosen experiments become the foundation of the entire superstructure'. Theoretical developments in the sciences can be unbounded by anything except contradictions, but they only achieve the status of being proven, applicable, when they line up with the physical world: until then they are abstractions.

A doctoral student of mine spent over three years in solving a particular set of equations defining a non-uniform series of flow conditions. Weekly tutorials encouraged him to keep going until the day when he presented me with a sheet of graph paper on which he had drawn the results of his solution. 'Very good,' I further encouraged him, 'but, of course we must prove the theory if it is to be useful.' It was a very disconsolate student who went away to build his experiment. But he did, and the experimental results appeared in due course on a similar piece of graph paper. Within the limits of experimental error, they lined up with the theory. (He was awarded his PhD by a discerning examiner on the basis of just one line in the mathematical development! It was just as important though, to be able to say that the outstanding mathematics produced realistic results that harmonised with observation.)

In his autobiographical notes, written in 1949, Einstein wrote that 'the revolution begun by the introduction of the [electromagnetic] field was by no means finished'. Evidently, much remains to be done before we can claim that science has conquered all or that we have in our hands the *how* of creation. Even then, we still have to cross the threshold of the *why*.

*　　*　　*

Whether we have realistic scientific theories or not, or are likely to get them, they will be limited. Hawking has said that they are 'just mathematical models, [existing] only in our minds'. They might not finally be realistic in an absolute sense — only realistic within our limited perception. Even the realism for which Copernicus strove is thus eventually limited. In that case, how far do they go in leading us towards God?

Galen was a second-century Greek, a physician raised in the philosophical climate of Greece, whose writings, incidentally, were studied by Galileo as a medical student in his undergraduate days. He held that 'the purpose of a deity could be ascertained by detailed inspection of his assumed works in nature'. His philosophy encouraged the seeker to discover as much as possible of the formation and working of the cosmos: through this he would surely detect the fingerprint of God and thus his intentions. William Paley didn't have that confidence: 'The so-called laws of nature may be, even now, nothing more than a way of codifying observations that have been made.' It was Max Planck, the founder of quantum theory, who said, 'Science cannot solve the ultimate mystery of nature.'

In short, scientific theories, no matter how realistic they may be in our perception, cannot be the proof of God's existence. And that seems reasonable, for scientific theories come and go. It would be a great mistake to hang on to a piece of science as proof for the existence of God, or even of his plan, the *why*. Should the scientific statement be superseded, there remains no basis for the proof of God or his plan. We cannot use something of a natural, transient nature to support someone of a spiritual, eternal nature. The heavens may declare the glory of the Lord but, while they are good evidence, they aren't the proof of his existence.

An example of the problem that can result from such misplaced loyalty is seen in the Shroud of Turin. For many who assumed it to be the burial shroud of Jesus, it has been a source of inspiration, even a focus of faith: *this* was the proof for Christ. The recent revelation that it is a thirteenth-century piece of cloth has undermined the proposition of a real Jesus to any who leaned upon the Shroud for absolute evidence.

Robert Boyle, chemist and thermodynamicist, related the material and the spiritual world well. Using the watch as his example, he saw the world as a mechanism. But he also saw further. Barrow and Tipler describe this: 'Although immediate efficient causes of phenomena were entirely mechanical in Boyle's physics, their ultimate and final causes were seen as entirely supernatural.' A spiritual dimension was something above and beyond the physical realm in which he made himself famous. The spiritual dimension was there — and it pointed to God.

*   *   *

This leads us to a riddle surrounding the physics of the cosmos and consequently all scientific disciplines. Although these scientific expressions don't tell us the *why* of God or bring us directly into the supernatural dimension of which Boyle spoke, why, since they are such strong pointers, is there a great gulf fixed between science and Christianity? They both search for the things of God, but an onlooker would be excused for saying that these two great institutions are on divergent courses.

The root of this separation goes back to the Galileo Affair when the church and Galileo were lined up against each other in a battle which Galileo lost but for which the church has paid ever since. Cynical historians have used the judgement on Galileo, 'vehemently suspected of heresy' as typical of a reactionary religious attitude, a church more interested in defending its own privileged position than identifying with a real world. No doubt, the Luddite spirit lurked in the corridors of power whose closed doors Galileo was rattling, but they weren't the corridors of the church until much later. In consequence, to hold up Galileo as the champion of an intellectual humanism at war with a set of religious buffoons is incorrect.

There were several contributory features leading to the great division and one of the most important was Galileo himself. A man of great intellect with the capacity of a clear thinker, he was unusually powerful in portraying his arguments in a form that made them unanswerable. The thought experiments he undertook had a devastating strength: for example, he didn't need the experiments with gravity, dropping balls from a tower, to prove that acceleration was a function of the gravitational attraction, not of the weight of an object — his arguments left no alternative.

A fast, clear mind can be a disadvantage — and it was to Galileo. He didn't suffer fools gladly and while he attracted admirers, he also created many enemies and displayed an acerbic nature towards those who opposed him. These were his own university colleagues, fearful perhaps that their lecture notes, based on an Aristotelianism learned by rote, might be out of date (the last thing a university lecturer wants to do is to spend time updating his notes!). Further, this was a period when research was not a driving force in the university scene — professional advancement did not depend on the number of papers produced by an individual — and so original thought was not high on the agenda. Galileo was therefore an uncomfortable inclusion on a faculty list. And then, within the conservative environment of the academic world, his touch of flamboyance in demonstrating his proofs in experiment would have further enraged his peers.

This was the breeding ground for the first opposition that Galileo was to encounter. It was from his own academic community that there was formed the *Liga*, a secret resistance movement described in a letter to Galileo as 'a band of malevolent persons who are jealous of your qualities and achievements and who gather together in the house of the Archbishop [of Florence] seeking madly to find something with which to discredit you'.

But Galileo had another problem in himself: he was a hopeless politician. His decisions were politically disastrous.

His observations in 1609 and 1610 were made in Padua where, since 1592, he had held the Chair of Mathematics. Padua was within the Republic of Venice. Under the rule of the Doge of Venice, Galileo was safe from any outside interference from Rome or elsewhere. It was the Doge to whom Galileo had presented his first telescope and who had, in consequence, favoured Galileo with a lifetime appointment and doubled salary at the University. He could have spent the remainder of his life in the Republic in safety and in an affluence to which academics were (are!) unaccustomed, but he resigned his position to return to Tuscany for an appointment as Chief Mathematician and Philosopher to the Duke of Tuscany. This was an altogether more exposed position, as it turned out.

In his controversy with the *Liga*, Galileo allowed himself to be drawn from his scientific arena into theology. In this, he was outwitted by his opponents and when he had been tempted to this different and unfamiliar ground, his was a lost cause.

He made another political mistake in the deployment of his case. He argued the Copernican cause without recourse to the work of Kepler and thus without some of the finest evidence to hand. It was the use solely of his own observations that may have revealed another side to his character — egocentricity — which is hinted at in his pompous declaration of his sighting the moons of Jupiter (see chapter 3). He wanted to prove Copernicus — by himself and without help — not standing on the shoulders of giants. The 'Not Invented Here' syndrome, in which the work of all others is ignored, is familiar in all fields of research and has evidently been around for a long while. It still stalks among the coffee cups in every university common room and research establishment.

Galileo was clearly a man with passions similar to all of us, yet there was another side to him to which, in a moment, we shall turn.

What of his opponents? They were initially the university professors, loosely formed into an opposition, the *Liga*, centred in Florence. But they weren't strong enough: they needed a cat's paw and the church was it. In 1611, there was the first hint that the argument was being widened to include theological aspects. In 1614, a sermon preached in Florence was a shot across the bows to Galileo. Without mentioning him by name, it was aimed at marshalling public opinion against Galileo. 'All mathematicians' were branded as 'agents of the devil, who ought to be banned from Christendom' (a sentiment sometimes heard from undergraduate quarters in examination rooms, even today).

But Galileo knew how to play to the gallery. He had carefully cultivated his public, an intelligent and alert section of Italian society, by writing not in the academic language of the day, Latin, but in the indigenous Italian which could be understood outside of the university walls. When, in 1615, Rome became involved through a complaint written from Florence that the 'Galiesti', the supporters of Galileo, were undermining the Scriptures, Galileo was also careful enough to court the support of Rome.

This alleged denial of Scripture became a focus in the debate. It was inevitable that an appeal would be made to the edict of the Council of Trent, claiming that interpretation of the Scripture was the prerogative of the church. While Galileo was not without his friends in the church, he had his enemies. In addition, the church had its problems. In particular, Luther and Calvin had destroyed the monolithic structure. Had that not happened, putting Rome in a defensive position against anything that might weaken it further, the judgement meted out on 22nd June 1633 on Galileo might have been far more lenient, even to the point of accommodating his views as a hypothesis, a fairly standard dodge. Instead, he was 'condemned to imprisonment at the pleasure of the Holy Congregation, and ordered not to treat further, in whatever manner, either in words or in writing, of the mobility of the Earth and the stability of the Sun; otherwise he [would] incur the penalty of relapse. The book entitled the *Dialogue on the Two Principal World Systems — Ptolemaic and Copernican* [was] to be prohibited.'

*   *   *

The power struggle had been complex and all the weaknesses of man were everywhere evident — ambition, envy and pride, vying with territorial defence in both the secular and religious spheres. In this atmosphere an unjust judgement on Galileo was inevitable. One thing was obscured by this tragedy though; that is, the place of respect in which Galileo held the Scriptures he was accused of undermining — and this shows us the other side of the man.

At the beginning of a letter written to Madame Christina of Lorraine, Grand Duchess of Tuscany, Galileo made his point: 'I think in the first place that it is very pious to say and prudent to affirm that the Holy Bible can never speak untruth — whenever its true meaning is understood.... The Bible was designed to persuade men of those articles and propositions which, surpassing all human reason, could not be made credible by science, or by any other means than through the mouth of the Holy Spirit.' Putting the work of the Bible and of the Holy Spirit into context, Galileo affirmed that the Bible was not only inspired by the Holy Spirit but was written with 'the primary purpose of the salvation of souls and the service of God'. 'The intention of the Holy Ghost is to teach us how one gets to heaven, not how the heavens go,' a quotation he took from a cardinal of his day.

Galileo saw two books laid out before him. One was 'this grand book of the Universe, which stands continually open to our gaze [which] ... cannot be understood unless one learns to comprehend the language and read the alphabet in which it is composed. It is written in the language of mathematics ... without which it is humanly impossible to understand a single word of it'. The other was the Bible. The book of Nature and the Book of Scripture were, to Galileo, complementary not contradictory, since they emanated from the same author. Thus, in a letter of January 1633, exactly five months before the verdict on his Copernicanism, and hence on his interpretation of the Bible, was read, Galileo wrote, 'Thus the world is the work and the scriptures the word of the same God.' Truth is one.

This was not a sterile, theoretical or even politically expedient view that he held. The author of both books was, to Galileo, a reality who intervened in his life and with whom he was engaged in a relationship. In family matters, for example, he saw the hand of God. To his father he wrote in 1590 of a particular problem: 'In this matter it is perhaps more than in others important to pray to God that it may please him to dispose in the best way possible.'

This sense of personal relationship with God was intended as an encouragement to professional colleagues. Writing to Marcus Welser in 1612, he said, 'But in whatever way we spend our lives we ought to receive them as the highest gift from the hands of God who might have done nothing for us at all. First and foremost we should receive them not only with thanks but in infinite gratitude for his goodness ... [that] leads us upwards to that which is celestial and divine.'

That sense of a walk with, and love for, the 'Divine Artificer' was evident both in the frequent gratitude he devoutly offered to God in his writings and in the personal letters he exchanged with his daughter, Maria Celeste, in the convent where her Christian life was expressed.

In his final days, Galileo could be found, still under house arrest, rapidly going blind, yet noting the libations of the moon, continuing research on sound as well as clock mechanisms — and being carried, in his physical infirmity, to a local chapel to meet with his God.

Professor Wallace, an academic and philosopher from Washington DC, summing up the life of Galileo, wrote of 'Galileo's striking testimony, written large in the events of 1633 and their aftermath, [so] that being a scientist need not preclude one's having a strong religious faith, and that is surely a potent lesson for our time'.

CHAPTER ELEVEN

AN OCEAN OF TRUTH

THE SEARCH IS ON for the mind of God.

A strategy is laid out by Stephen Hawking in the last paragraph of his book *A Brief History of Time*. 'However, if we should discover a complete theory ... we shall ... be able to take part in the discussion of the question of why it is that we and the Universe exist. If we find the answer to that it will be the ultimate triumph of human reason — for then we would know the mind of God.'

As I have attempted to show, though, there is no automatic route from the *how* to the *why*. Educational as it is to investigate how things happen, why they do is in another dimension. Yet Hawking has revealed something in the heart of us all: a quest to know what is 'out there', not just those things that are within the compass of our telescopes or our mathematics, but a transcendent force of life, if it exists. Is such a search within the domain of the cosmologist or the scientist — or is anybody qualified to pursue this investigation? Certainly, Stephen Hawking sees the scientist deeply involved, but he also recognises that this is a task for everyone, 'philosophers, scientists and just ordinary people'.

At the beginning of his book *Cosmos*, Carl Sagan, who wrote the Introduction to *A Brief History of Time*, says, 'The Cosmos is all that is or ever was or ever will be.' It is the brave statement of a fixed mind, not that of a researcher, an investigator in a world where Einstein said that the revolution was by no means finished. For Einstein, as for Hawking, there was still discovery to be made.

Yet the layman's view of the scientist makes Sagan's position archetypal: atheistic and certain of his position, presenting his views with the assurance of one who presumably has the supporting facts to hand. That this is not the inevitable stance of the scientist is seen in the lives of the men whose work we have been tracing.

The major advances in cosmology have been via a lineage that included Aristotle and Ptolemy, whose erroneous geocentric universe was altered and refined by a series of men beginning with Copernicus. The giants upon whose shoulders Newton stood were Copernicus, Brahe, Kepler and Galileo. Classical physics was established by that direct line, to which undoubtedly many others made their contribution. The new physics began in the mind of Michael Faraday, was formalised by James Clerk-Maxwell and expanded by Einstein's theories of relativity. At the same time, Max Planck was developing the concept of quanta so that, together, relativity and quantum mechanics painted a new picture.

As I began the work leading to this book, I was struck by a feature of many of these men that I had not appreciated before. Between Ptolemy and Einstein there is an unbroken series of those for whom pioneering science was not a deterrent but a magnet, drawing them to God. They all not only acknowledged the existence of God, but sought him and, in some measure, claimed a relationship with him in their lives. Others, as we have seen, spoke of him or the dimension that includes him, either directly or indirectly: 'God does not play dice'; 'Science cannot solve the ultimate mystery of nature.'

To avoid mistaking what is behind the scientist's statement, we must acknowledge that the word 'God' is not always used to refer to an ultimate, divine being who is called Creator. The Greek philosopher, Anaxagoras, had a repository for unsolved problems: he called it 'mind'. He earned the sarcasm of Aristotle who said that Anaxagoras used this as an excuse whenever he was puzzled over the explanation of something. In nineteenth-century writing it became fashionable to use 'God' as the convenient repository into which unsolved problems and unknown factors could be put until they were rescued by scientific discoveries that explained them.

This was not the case with the line of giants we have listed. Copernicus sincerely declared his faith in Christ — God personalised in Jesus Christ — and was, moreover, a canon in the Cathedral of Fraudenberg. He did not become a priest within his church, so this could have been a nominal commitment to make

Copernicus' studies easier. But it wasn't. His research, which he regarded as 'a loving duty to seek the truth in all things, in so far as God has granted that', led him to describe the cosmos as being 'built for us by the Best and Most Orderly Workman of all'. His conclusion was: 'The Universe has been built for us by a supremely good and orderly Creator.' Nearly five hundred years of further research has revealed the order.

Tycho Brahe was motivated, in part, in his measurements of the heavens because of a problem he had in squaring Copernicus' model with Scripture. His solution, a geometry that included the earth at the centre of the universe around which the sun revolved while all the other planets themselves orbited the sun, was a clear compromise between his own measurements and his traditional understanding of the Bible. He was mistaken, but it is an indication of the influence that his Christian life had on him.

The stoic nature of Kepler and the recognition that his life was in God's hands has already been mentioned. To him, the cosmos was a 'sacred sermon, a veritable hymn to God the Creator'. He admitted that he had constantly prayed to God that he might succeed in his calculations if what Copernicus said was true — and he had the testimony that divine providence did intervene.

We have seen Galileo's dependency on God at different levels of life, his family, his colleagues, his science. Newton, too, allowed his convictions of God's direct interest to permeate his science. In his book *Optics*, his position on the creation was clearly stated:

> It seems probable to me that God in the beginning formed matter in solid, massy, hard, impenetrable particles, of such size and figures, and with such other properties, in such proportions to space, as most conduced to the end for which he formed them; even so very hard as never to wear or break in pieces.

Faraday's perception of the spiritual life was reflected in a lecture he gave in 1854: 'High as man is placed above the creatures around him, there is a higher and far more exalted position within his view.' He continued, speaking of the 'hope set before us, as if man, by reasoning, could find out God.... I have never seen anything incompatible between those things of man which can be known by the spirit of man which is within him and those higher things concerning his future, which he cannot know by that spirit'.

As a student at Cambridge, James Clerk-Maxwell became a Christian. The profound effect on his personal life can be understood from correspondence with his wife: 'May the Lord preserve you from all the evil that assaults you, to work out his purposes. Think what God has decided to do to all those who submit themselves to his righteousness and are willing to receive his gift. They are to be conformed to the image of his son.' But this wasn't a private affair for the Maxwell household. Visitors to his laboratory were invited to, and impressed by, the morning prayer meetings he led and his fame as a Christian was evidenced in the obituary notice in *Nature* magazine: 'His simple Christian faith gave him a peace too deep to be ruffled by bodily pain or external circumstances.'

It would be wrong to suggest that these men all had the same level of Christian commitment: they did not. Following a lecture at the Royal Institution on one occasion, Faraday was reputed to have been missing during the vote of thanks from the Prince Regent: he had slipped off to a prayer meeting! But Newton, at the end of his life, still wondered if 'a great ocean of truth' had not been just beyond his reach.

Yet we can note this. For these men, irrespective of the depth of their relationship with Christ, there was no conflict in recognising the reality of God while they stood at the frontiers of scientific endeavour. And this was not a God who was an excuse for ignorance, nor was it one who had set the universe in motion, only to retire to a safe distance while it wound its way down through time. This was the God with whom there was clearly some direct level of communication. Can we take their word, as we have taken their science, attempting to stand on their shoulders, or do we take the affirmation, 'The cosmos is all'?

Carl Sagan is not alone in his position and it would be foolish to suggest that scientists are apt to be Christian. Laplace, whose reductionism we have noted, having written his book *Mécanique Celeste,* presented a copy to Napoleon. There ensued a famous exchange as Napoleon addressed what he considered an oversight in Laplace's work: 'You have written this huge book on the system of the world without once mentioning the author of the universe.'

'Sire,' Laplace responded, 'I have no need for that hypothesis.'

In a subsequent conversation with another mathematician,

Joseph-Louis Lagrange, Napoleon mentioned this. Lagrange replied, 'But that is a fine hypothesis. It explains so many things.'

Whom, then, do we believe — the men who prayed or the men who did not need the hypothesis?

The second group is epitomised by the Russian cosmonauts who, having made their space-shot, reported that they had looked for God but hadn't found him — he wasn't there. The first group says the opposite, turning theory into reality by 'well chosen experiments' as Galileo recommended.

Black holes feature in cosmology and have done so in my presentation. The person who says, 'Black holes do not exist because I have never seen one,' is not likely to be taken seriously — he rejects the black hole for the wrong reason while ignoring the evidence. At the same time, that a theoretical system has yet to be proved in the world of phenomena does not speak against the black hole, only our knowledge of it. On the other hand, the seriousness with which we receive a claim, 'I've located a black hole,' depends not on our experience of black holes or even on his previous connection with them, but on the credibility rating of the speaker — his track record.

So it was with Robert Boyle. He was a founder of the Royal Society in London — possibly the most prestigious scientific society in the world — and, since he lifted chemistry from the status of alchemy to that of a science, was sometimes called the father of modern chemistry. His track-record earned him a reputation as the greatest physical scientist of his generation. Beyond the physi- cal world that he was uncovering, Boyle saw a spiritual dimension. He regarded this with such importance that he instituted a series of lectures in London for others to learn of it.

Over the years that Lord Kelvin held the Chair of Natural Philosophy at the University of Glasgow, he began the first lecture of every day by leading his students in prayer to God, regularly asking 'that all our doings may be ordered by thy divine governance'. Kelvin, the founder of thermodynamics, was searching out the mind of God.

That illustrious line of scientists, whose track-records are established in the brilliance that has shaped our understanding of the cosmos, also includes those whose admission is, 'I have located a spiritual dimension transcending the physical sciences.' Of course, there are those who say that this particular world of phenomena has not become part of their experience. Few are rash enough to say, as the Russian scientists, 'Because I've not seen it, it doesn't exist.' Among other things they undermine is the philosophy of virtually all of today's research in the theoretical sciences.

Black holes have taught us that seeing is not necessarily believing. They are a lesson in faith.

One thing we can conclude: if knowing a person's mind arises out of knowing the person, these men certainly had access to the mind of God. All else was, at best, knowing about him as I might know about an artist by the art he produces.

*   *   *

Was it because they searched the heavens that these men discovered heavenly things — or is this relationship for ordinary people too?

Blaise Pascal was one of the great mathematicians of history and a man of common sense. He described the theory of probabilities, a mathematically rigorous means of determining the chances of an event taking place, as 'at bottom only common sense reduced to calculation: it makes us appreciate with exactitude what reasonable minds feel by a sort of instinct'. Following his death, a paper was found sewn into his coat. The paper had become a constant, secret companion, carefully hidden in the lining of one jacket after another as he changed them. The paper was a description of an event of such value in Pascal's life that he never shared it openly.

> God of Abraham, God of Isaac, God of Jacob, not of philosophers and scholars. Certitude. Certitude. Joy. Feeling. Peace. God of Jesus Christ. My God and thy God. 'Thy God shall be my God.' Forgetfulness of the world and of everything, except God. He is to be found only by the ways taught by the Gospel. Greatness of the soul of man. 'Righteous Father, the world hath not known Thee, but I have known Thee.' Joy, joy, joy, tears of joy.... Total submission to Jesus Christ.

Pascal's revelation brought him to a knowledge of the God he recognised in Jesus Christ, by a way other than that of philosophers and scholars, but to be found in the gospel of the Bible he loved. The result was an assurance that gave joy, peace, certitude. He knew God.

In the twentieth century there is no shortage of scientists and ordinary people who have found this route to the mind of God. Each has his own testimony resulting from his well-chosen experiment. From a position of practical atheism, though not expressed as dynamically as Carl Sagan's, my conversion in Cambridge also brought the response of heart that Pascal described.

But this was not the emotion of a moment. It was the beginning of a daily relationship, expressed however imperfectly, in which it was possible to know the mind of God. There had been moments when the view of Saturn in the eyepiece of my son's telescope had been impaired by the prevailing turbulence, but others when it had been breathtakingly clear, yet the telescope continued pointing at Saturn. This expresses the relationship I've discovered in God. Quite simply expressed, it is pointing myself at Jesus Christ — to know him and through that, the mind of God. As with Galileo and others it has continued, not as a theoretical proposition — a possibility like a black hole or a Big Bang — but in an application to daily life among family, friends, colleagues and in the pursuit of a profession. Further, it has given an assurance that in the area which cannot be probed by the scientists' instruments and physics — beyond the spacetime boundary which we shall call eternity, there is the continuation of that relationship.

'Thy God shall be my God.... Total submission to Jesus Christ ... eternally in joy.'

* * *

The title of this book includes eternity as a consideration. We have seen how there was a boundary condition at the singularity called creation. Before that, there was neither space nor time. We conclude from the Second Law of thermodynamics that there will, in the normal course of events, be a moment when entropy has done what Clausius predicted. It will have reached a maximum: time will be no more because entropy cannot increase further.

Outside these boundaries, we have no scientific instrument to help us discover what exists. What we can conclude is that the Second Law cannot prevail, since that would demand a time arrow where there is no time. The only word we have for a domain where there is no Second Law, no decay, no increase in disorder, is eternity.

Eternity is nature's destiny because of the arbitration of the Second Law. But eternity which is only the consequence of natural events would be a pretty boring place, a universe in a petrified state with no life or means of living. Is the end to be at an entropy maximum? We had no scientific means of defining the creation moment and we similarly have no way of predicting the end: God may not wait for a state of maximum entropy to occur. His intervention would introduce a different eternity. Certainly there would be no decay, but this eternity would go beyond the scientifically measurable, the *how*, to the *why*.

Einstein was convinced that, even in a quantum event, there is a further level of understanding from which an occurrence may be dictated. If we are also convinced, we may conclude that the creation needed a Creator, God, who inhabited eternity. If God had made friends with Copernicus and Clerk-Maxwell, Kepler and Kelvin, as well as others — philosophers, scientists and ordinary people — is he likely to terminate that friendship simply because entropy has become intolerably high? Is eternity simply his lofty, isolated residence? An answer to that lies with the epitaph to Galileo Galilei, written on his death by his student, Viviani: 'With philosophic and Christian firmness he rendered up his soul to his Creator, sending it, as he liked to believe, to enjoy and to watch from a closer vantage point those eternal and immutable marvels which he, by means of a fragile device, had brought closer to our mortal eyes with such eagerness and impatience.'

BIBLIOGRAPHY

The following is a list of associated literature. Many but not all of these titles are referred to in the body of the book.

M Allen-Olney, *The Private Life of Galileo* (London, 1870).

PW Atkins, *The Second Law* (Scientific American Library).

JD Barrow and J Silk, *The Left Hand of Creation* (Counterpoint, 1983).

JD Barrow and FJ Tipler, *The Anthropic Cosmological Principle* (Oxford University Press: Oxford, 1988).

ET Bell, *Men of Mathematics* (Simon and Schuster: London, 1962).

CB Boyer, *A History of Mathematics* (Princeton University Press: Princeton, NJ, 1968).

WW Bryant, 'Galileo', *Pioneers of Progress, Men of Science*, (SPCK: London, 1920).

Sir D Brewster, *The Life of Sir Isaac Newton* (Gall and Inglis).

HA Bruck, GV Coyne and MS Longair, *Astrophysical Cosmology: Proc. of the Study Week on Cosmology and Fundamental Physics* (Pontificia Academia Scientiarum, 1983).

RE Butts and JC Pitt, *New Perspectives on Galileo* (D. Reidel Publishing Company, 1978).

RP Crease and CC Mann, *The Second Creation* (Collier/Macmillan: London, 1986).

JB Cohen, *Revolution in Science* (Harvard University Press: Cambridge, MA, 1985).

GV Coyne, SJM Heller and J Zycinski, *The Galileo Affair: A Meeting of Faith and Science* (Specola Vaticana, 1985).

AC Crombie, 'Galileo, Galilei: A Philosophical Symbol' (Act. Congr. Int. Hist, Sci. vol 8 (1956) pp. 1089–1095.

C Darwin, *The Origin of Species* (William Benton, Encyclopaedia Brittanica Inc: London).

C Darwin, *The Descent of Man* (William Benton, Encyclopaedia Brittanica Inc: London).

P Davies, *The New Physics* (Cambridge University Press: London 1989).

P Davies, *God and the New Physics* (Penguin: London 1983).

P Davies, *Superforce* (Simon and Schuster: London 1984).

R Dawkins, *The Blind Watchmaker* (Penguin: London 1986).

M Denton, *Evolution, A Theory in Crisis* (Burnett: London, 1985).

S Drake, *Galileo at Work* (University of Chicago Press: Chicago, Il, 1978).

D Gooding and FAJL James, *Faraday Rediscovered* (Stockton Press, 1985).

Sir AH Eddington, *The Nature of the Physical World* (Cambridge, 1953).

L Fermi and G Bernardini, *Galileo and the Scientific Revolution* (Premier Books, 1961).

ER Harrison, *Cosmology* (Cambridge University Press: Cambridge 1988).

SW Hawking, *A Brief History of Time* (Bantam Books: London, 1988).

C Hyers, *The Meaning of Creation* (John Knox Press: Atlanta, GA, 1984).

MF Kaplan, *Homage to Galileo* (MIT Press: London, 1965).

AG King, *Kelvin the Man* (Hodder and Stoughton: London, 1925).

A Koestler, 'The Greatest Scandal in Christendom', *Critic*, vol 23 (1964), pp 14–20.

A Koestler, *The Sleepwalkers: A History of Man's Changing Vision of the Universe* (Hutchinson: London / Macmillan: New York, 1959).

D Layzer, *Constructing the Universe* (Scientific American Library, 1984).

R Learner, *Astronomy through the Telescope* (Van Norstrand Reinhold: Wokingham, 1981).

HM Morris, *The Biblical Basis for Modern Science* (Baker: Grand Rapids, Mi, 1984).

HM Morris, *Biblical Cosmology and Modern Science* (Presbyterian and Reformed Publishing Company: Phillipsburg, NJ, 1982).

HM Morris, *Men of Science, Men of God* (Master Books: 1988).

HM Morris, *Science and the Bible* (Scripture Press: Amersham, 1988).

HM Morris and JC Whitcombe, *The Genesis Flood* (Evangelical Press: Welwyn, 1969).

L Motz and JH Weaver, *The Concepts of Science* (Plenum Press: London 1988).

HZ Pagels, *Perfect Symmetry* (Bantam Books: London, 1986).

W Paley, *Natural Theology* (Baldwyn and Company, 1819).

R Palter, *1666 — The Annus Mirabilis of Sir Isaac Newton* (MIT Press: London, 1970).

C Papanastassion, *The Struggle of Science Against Superstition — Galileo* (in Greek — Papazissie: Athens, 1950). (Rev. by Alk Mazis: Arch. Int. Hist. Sci., vol 4 (1951), pp 213–217.)

SP Parker, *McGraw-Hill Encyclopaedia of Astronomy* (McGraw-Hill Book Company: Maidenhead, 1982).

HO Peitgen and PH Richter, *The Beauty of Fractals* (Springer-Verlag: Berlin, 1986).

HO Peitgen and D Saupe, *The Science of Fractals* (Springer-Verlag: Berlin, 1988).

G de Santillano, *The Crime of Galileo* (University of Chicago Press: Chicago, Il, 1955).

RJ Seeger, *Galileo Galilei — His Life and His Works* (Pergamon Press: Oxford, 1966).

D Shapere, *Galileo — A Philosophical Study* (Chicago University Press: Chicago, Il, 1974).

R Shapiro, *Origins* (Bantam Books: London 1987).

F Sherwood Taylor, *Galileo and the Freedom of Thought* (Watts: London, 1938).

J Schwinger, *Einstein's Legacy* (Scientific American Library, 1986).

CB Thaxton, WL Bradley and RL Olson, *The Mystery of Life's Origin* (Philosophical Library: New York, NY, 1986).

Sir W Thompson, *Popular Lectures and Addresses* (MacMillan: London, 1891).

JS Trefil, *From Atoms to Quarks* (Charles Scribner's Sons: New York, NY, 1980).

JS Trefil, *Space Time Infinity* (Smithsonian Books: Washington DC, 1985).

HJ Van Till, DA Young and C Menningra, *Science Held Hostage* (Intervarsity Press: Downers Grove, Il, 1988).

J Weister, *The Genesis Connection* (Thomas Nelson: Nashville, TN, 1983).

EJ Young, *Studies in Genesis One* (Presbyterian and Reformed Publishing Company: Phillipsburg, NJ).

INDEX

WITHDRAWN